Valuing the Environment

Valuing the Environment
Economic Approaches to Environmental Evaluation

Proceedings of a Workshop held at
Ludgrove Hall, Middlesex Polytechnic
on 13 and 14 June 1990

Edited by Annabel Coker
and Cathy Richards

Belhaven Press
London and Florida

© Flood Hazard Research Centre, 1992

First published in Great Britain in 1992 by
Belhaven Press (a division of Pinter Publishers Limited)
25 Floral Street, London WC2E 9DS

British Library Cataloguing in Publication Data

A CIP catalogue record for this book is available from the
British Library

ISBN 1 85293 212 0

Distributed in North America by
CRC Press, 2000 Corporate Blvd. N.W.,
Boca Raton, Florida, 33431

HC
79
E5
V34
1992

Library of Congress Cataloging-in-Publication Data

Valuing the environment : economic approaches to environmental
    evaluation : proceedings of a workshop held at Ludgrove Hall,
    Middlesex Polytechnic, on 13th and 14th of June 1990 / edited by
    Annabel Coker and Cathy Richards.
        p.   cm.
    Includes bibliographical references and index.
    ISBN 1-85293-212-0
    1. Environmental policy—Costs—Congresses.   2. Environmental
protection—Costs—Congresses.   I. Coker, Annabel, 1948–
II. Richards, Cathy, 1947–
HC79.E5V262   1992
333.7′2—dc20   91-46605
                                                              CIP

Photoset in North Wales by
Derek Doyle & Associates, Mold, Clwyd.
Printed and bound in Great Britain by
Biddles Ltd, Guildford and King's Lynn.

Contents

List of figures

List of tables

Preface

In many fields of environmental studies increased attention is being paid to ways of valuing the environment, particularly in monetary terms. Yet many ecologists are far from happy even with evaluating different components of the environment in relative terms. But unless we use monetary value as a common means of indicating relative values how, for example, are we to make decisions on the relative importance of the loss of an archaeological site compared with the potential gains in wildlife from new habitats resulting from a coastal engineering scheme?

This volume is the result of a multi-disciplinary workshop held by Middlesex Polytechnic's Flood Hazard Research Centre in May 1990 which was designed to bring together economists and ecologists working in the field of coastal management. The workshop addressed various issues raised by the problem of how to value coastal environments. One benefit of joint discussions is the opportunity they provide for clarifying terminology and arriving at agreed definitions of terms in common usage such as the distinction between 'evaluation' and 'valuation'. It is also helpful to ensure the precise usage of the terms 'ecological' and 'environmental' and to recognise that they should not be used interchangeably (these distinctions are clarified in Chapter 1).

The workshop developed from the Research Centre's research for the Ministry of Agriculture, Fisheries and Food, the Coast Protection and Sea Defence Research Project (COPRES), to devise better methods for assessing the costs and benefits of coast protection (i.e. erosion control at the coast) and sea defence (i.e. the alleviation of coastal flooding). These methods are needed so that comparisons of the costs and benefits of coastal schemes can incorporate all relevant environmental considerations.

If the success of a workshop can be judged by the intensity of debate, then this one was a success. The combination of different attitudes to the environment and strongly held opinions resulted in some lively discussion, in spite of occasional confusion caused by the use of specialists' jargon. By using the terms 'ecologists' and 'economists' in summarising discussions we do not mean to convey the impression of two groups of protagonists; rather the terms have been used for convenience. Not all the participants could be described, or would wish to be described, as being either ecologists or economists. Neither is it wished to imply that either of these groupings in any way represented a homogenous entity – disagreements occurred as frequently within as between groups.

One of the main achievements of this workshop was the bringing together of specialists from disparate backgrounds to clarify the issues relating both to the present situation as regards environmental evaluation and site assessment; and to the direction of future research. It is hoped that the 'ecologists' felt that they had been able to contribute to the debate by indicating both what is at issue and the relative usefulness of different decision aids. The 'economists' may now have a clearer view of areas where agreement is possible and of those areas in which they should 'tread with care'.

Many people deserve our thanks for assisting in the preparations for the workshop and the production of this volume. Celine Ottmann organised the workshop with great care for detail; the staff of Ludgrove Hall (Middlesex Polytechnic) provided the right environment for our discussions; the authors provided their papers; Ian Slavin and Nick Beesley prepared the diagrams with great skill and speed; and Josie Difrancesco provided valuable assistance with wordprocessing. The authors have attempted to do justice to the workshop by editing the disparate contributions into a coherent volume.

Annabel Coker and Cathy Richards
Flood Hazard Research Centre
1991

Acronyms

AONB   Area of Outstanding Natural Beauty
BCA   Benefit-Cost Analysis
CBA   Cost-Benefit Analysis
COPRES Coast Protection and Sea Defence Research Project
CPA   Coast Protection Authority
CVM   Contingent Valuation Method
EA   Environmental Assessment
EEC   European Economic Community
EIA   Environmental Impact Assessment
EN   English Nature
ESA   Environmentally Sensitive Area
MAFF   Ministry of Agriculture, Fisheries and Food
MPFHRC Middlesex Polytechnic Flood Hazard Research Centre
NCC   Nature Conservancy Council
NNR   National Nature Reserve
NRA   National Rivers Authority
OED   Oxford English Dictionary
RSPB   Royal Society for the Protection of Birds
SACTRA Standing Advisory Committee on Trunk Road Assessment
SPA   Special Protection Area
SSSI   Site of Special Scientific Interest
TCM   Travel Cost Method
TEV   Total Economic Value
WTA   Willingness to Accept
WTP   Willingness to Pay

1 'The devil and the deep blue sea'?

Edmund Penning-Rowsell

Introduction

Much is expected, today, of both economists and ecologists. When they meet, even more is expected of their wisdom in combination. Politicians want simple answers to difficult questions concerning ecological and environmental priorities, and better economic techniques for decision-making concerning investment in environmental improvement. 'More research is needed', as an answer, is no longer good enough.

But the questions *are* difficult. How much of the nation's scarce economic resources is to be efficiently spent in protecting nature reserves in coastal locations? Is it better to spend this money on a small number of key sites, or spread it more thinly over a wide range of habitats? What is the economic value of the feeding grounds of waders, or rare archaeological sites, or landscapes of historic and aesthetic significance? And, if we cannot answer these questions, will not the government (in the form of the Treasury) simply decline to invest these scarce resources in this way? – there are other competing demands for taxpayers' money.

Within our research on coast protection and sea defence it has become obvious that many of the benefits from investment in these fields are just those that are the most difficult – or perhaps impossible – to gauge and measure in money terms: the recreational experiences to be found at the coast, and the environmental values of coastal habitats and resources. In this respect the term ecological *evaluation* is used to refer to the relative evaluation of features of ecological interest, while the term economic *valuation* refers to attempts to place an economic value in monetary terms on such features.

So we face a problem: the costs of coast protection schemes – to protect buildings or nature conservation sites – are all too easily counted, but the key benefits are difficult to specify and value. But rather than conclude that assessing the benefits of coast protection and

1

sea defence should exclude these key benefits (which would distort resource allocation to a major degree) we decided that we should at least try to see how much common ground there was between economists and ecologists concerning whether such assessments were desirable and possible.

Our aim is to be provocative, but constructive. Thus, into this debate we have liberally sprinkled contributions from sceptics and a philosopher, to stir the pot of controversy. For if decision-makers understand fully the weaknesses in the concepts that underlie the data and techniques that they use, then at best they can tailor their decisions accordingly – by being suitably cautious – or, at worst, be better prepared for the inevitable criticisms that will come.

The specific objectives of this volume are:

- To bring together contributions from economists and ecologists in order to review any common ground there might be for environmental evaluation and monetary valuation.
- To evaluate critically the methodologies available for ecological evaluation and economic valuation of sites of nature conservation interest.
- To put forward procedural systems for coastal authorities (including the National River Authority) to use when planning coastal works which involve sites of nature conservation interest. In effect, these systems represent an implicit consensual evaluation and valuation of the environmental resources involved.

The papers in this volume echo the debates that we have had as researchers approaching coast protection and sea defence from a number of different disciplinary perspectives (ecology; geography; sociology; economics; archaeology). These debates have focused on decision-making at the interface between ecology and economics.

We recognise that there are no simple answers and that many dilemmas remain. There is the 'devil' on the one hand – universal economic quantification, leading us to an even more narrowly materialistic society. And there is the 'deep blue sea' on the other: letting the government – and specifically the Treasury – rule the waves by allowing them to make the environmental decisions for us when deciding on the criteria by which it gives grant aid for coastal works.

This volume therefore aims to air the problems of valuing environmental intangibles, and also the problems of *not* doing so. It arises out of a workshop which addressed the issue of valuing the ecological component of coastal environments. However, this aspect of the total environment cannot be considered in isolation from other environmental components. When a change is made that affects the ecological characteristics of an area, its other components – such as geological and archaeological characteristics and the uses it supports for agriculture or recreation – will usually be affected as well. Consideration of ecological value inevitably involves consideration of other values in the environment. The term 'environmental' will therefore be used here to refer to the whole 'package' of components which make up the environment, and the term 'ecological' will be restricted to the values of wildlife habitats and their supporting physical surroundings.

The debate we have joined

Government expenditure is increasingly scarce, since governments have decided that they should command and spend a decreasing share of the nation's gross domestic product. Almost all political parties now eschew policies that rely simply on increased taxation and government expenditure. Thus any government expenditure is seen to be made on behalf of a critical – if not antagonistic – public and attracts increasing scrutiny and increasingly rigorous requirements for its justification.

This justification can be of two types. First, there is justification based on political expediency or necessity, and this is not explicitly our concern although we recognise that governments have mandates to govern and to spend the nation's taxes. Or, second, there can be justification based on an assessment that the benefits to the nation from that expenditure outweigh its costs. Everyone recognises that the latter approach is not easy – and some say that it is impossible or downright misleading (see Adams, this volume) – but governments still require benefit-cost analyses to be done, in some form or another, to guide their decisions.

In this context decision-makers are increasingly confronted with the pressures to put economic values on environmental 'intangibles' such as wildlife and recreation experiences, in order that they may be taken into account when determining priorities for government when it is grant-aiding investment, in our case in coastal protection schemes. Furthermore, environmental investment itself is increasing, both in the water resources and coastal resources fields, and yet both decision-makers and their political masters are far from sure that they have the data and techniques that lead to decisions that give 'best value for money'.

Governments, moreover, are increasingly looking to economic instruments such as taxes and subsidies to achieve environmental objectives. In Britain this has led to the use of a number of such instruments, from payments to farmers in Environmentally Sensitive Areas (ESAs) to maintain low intensity agriculture on farms in the relevant areas of ecological or landscape significance, to major tax reductions for the use of unleaded petrol. In effect, the government is creating a market in environmental goods, but often without clear insights into the value of these goods. There is a pragmatic tendency to operate by trial and error, yet the sums involved are often large and sometimes huge, and a more systematic approach is to be desired.

The publication – and acceptance by the government – of 'The Pearce Report' (Pearce, Markandya and Barbier 1989) underlines the importance of this point from the decision-makers' perspectives. The report indicates the desire on the part of government for the development of methods and approaches to economic and monetary valuation of environmental goods, without giving explicit technical guidance on their development and practical application. Government acceptance of the concept of sustainability – the key environmental concept of the day – is also important, because it implies a trade-off between economic growth and the maintenance of, or improvement in, environmental values. But what are these values, and how can the trade-off be effected? The questions remain to be answered comprehensively.

In contrast to the Pearce approach, many environmentalists either feel that they do not have adequate information to make judgements even in relative terms about the importance of a site and rankings between sites, or that putting economic values on environmental goods and their intangible merits is not an appropriate way to take them into account. The latter perspective is often absolute and backed by moral judgements rather than concern for the inadequacy of technique and methods.

A key point about economic valuation in this context is that it requires a consensus, and this consensus, until now, has been missing. Without agreement between all concerned about the nature and extent of value, there can be no rational use of a numeraire such as money with which to weigh and compare goods. And such agreement or consensus needs to be based on an agreed knowledge base both concerning the nature of environmental resources, their prevalence or scarcity, and the effects on them of alternative policies. Identification, evaluation and valuation are all important stages in this process of building a knowledge base, but each is fraught with difficulty and controversy.

Particular appraisal problems at the coast

Appraisal of the economic and environmental effects of flooding and erosion at the coast raises particular evaluation issues. Not only are there the problems of evaluating 'environmental intangibles' such as the ecological and archaeological components and the recreational and amenity benefits of coastal sites and landscape features, but there are also institutional and conceptual difficulties.

First, institutional fragmentation at the coast hinders the development of a consensus about which policies should be adopted. The National Rivers Authority has a coastal protection and sea defence function, but also a duty to enhance and conserve environmental values. Other organisations involved in coastal-zone management include the District and County Councils – responsible for land-use planning, recreation and tourism and many other functions such as transportation and industrial development. There are also the navigation authorities responsible for port facilities, and nature conservation bodies such as English Nature and the National Trust. The list is lengthy and diverse. This fragmentation means that resource management at the coast is even more prone to conflict than elsewhere: each agency is pulling in a slightly different direction and this hinders progress towards some 'rational' plan for resource exploitation and nature conservation in the coastal zone. The different directions that these agencies are taking are an implicit reflection of their different valuations of the resources they are managing.

Second, coastal-zone management needs a regional perspective because plans and actions in one location can have a significant geomorphological effect 'downdrift'. Coastal resources are dynamic and interconnected and this undoubtedly hinders their evaluation and valuation. Externalities abound and this makes the efficient operation of a market in economic and environmental goods difficult; market failure will dominate and 'bad' decisions will predominate if these externalities are not taken into account. This is compounded in Britain because most of the decisions and most of the agencies operate at only a local level. This will inevitably mean that many of the knock-on effects of those decisions elsewhere are not even appreciated, let alone valued.

A third 'problem' at the coast is that the status quo is not natural or stable. Most resources at the coast – be they beaches for recreation or areas of significance for their nature conservation values – are a product of both natural geomorphological and hydrographic processes, and the result of many years of human intervention. Salt marshes, for example, are generally maintained by a complex combination of the natural forces of the tide and human use. Many nature reserves are protected from the open sea by banks and dykes constructed for other purposes, such as sea defence or erosion control.

This means that continued investment is often needed to maintain the status quo and retain the existing environmental values (in contrast to the situation away from the coast where much public sector investment – for example on motorways or reservoirs – is liable to harm nature conservation resources). This situation at the coast means that it is all the more important that some value can be put on environmental resources, because money may need to be spent – and justified – in their conservation through engineering or other schemes. The alternative is to let the coast evolve naturally from its current state, but that will mean major losses of environmental resources, as well as gains.

The complexity of this situation is illustrated by two of the examples discussed in this volume – Aldeburgh and Hengistbury Head. Whilst the engineering schemes adopted in these locations were justified on other grounds, a primary motivation for the coast-protection work was a desire to prevent environmental and heritage losses. In both cases, some contributors to this volume now feel that nature should have been allowed to take its course. However, the dilemma here is that these processes creating the erosion problems at the coast have been affected (or caused) by human interference with coastal processes 'up-drift', without which the problem would not have occurred in the first place. By this stance, letting nature take its course must be a general rule, not just one for areas where there is no property erosion.

In addition, fourth, coastal protection can involve trade-offs between aspects of the environment. Continued erosion is often desirable from a geological point of view, in order to reveal new sites and features, but this is seldom the case from an archaeological perspective. So decisions have to be made not simply between the protection of property versus the protection of the environment, or between the environmental values verses erosion, but also between different aspects of the environment.

Research into the benefits of coast protection and sea defence

This volume is one result of a research project undertaken at Middlesex Polytechnic between 1986 and 1991 which examined the methods and data required for assessing the benefits of schemes for coast protection (i.e. erosion control) and sea defence (i.e. flood alleviation). The other result of that research is a manual of techniques for the assessment of these benefits, representing the state of the art in benefit-cost analysis in this field.

The research has its antecedents in the very rudimentary requirements of the Department of the Environment (1984) for assessing the worthwhileness of these coastal-protection schemes, and the change in central government responsibility for coast protection from that Department to the Ministry of Agriculture, Fisheries and Food in 1985. Tighter project-appraisal systems were perceived as necessary, consequent upon that change of responsibility, and the research was commissioned to meet this need.

In the meantime, and before 1985, a number of coast protection and sea-defence schemes has aroused considerable controversy, focusing at least to some extent on the assessment of their beneficial effects. We were involved in assessing the economic viability of the Chesil sea-defence scheme (Penning-Rowsell and Parker 1987) which showed, for the first time, the nature of possible indirect effects of investment in flood alleviation at the coast.

A second study with which we were involved was the major controversy surrounding the Whitstable coast-protection and sea-defence scheme concerning the aesthetic impact on the town of major sea-walling proposals (Parker and Penning-Rowsell 1982), which resulted in a change of policy towards 'softer' defences, not least because the hard scheme was economically unviable. While no assessments of the landscape and recreational impacts of that scheme were undertaken, the controversy focused on those aspects of scheme design.

In addition to the 'environmental intangibles' analysed in this volume we have also studied the intangible effects of floods, in terms of their impact on the population at risk. Studies at Swalecliffe, Kent, and Uphill, Avon, showed that these intangible impacts can outweigh benefits measured as direct or indirect tangible flood damage to be avoided (Parker et al. 1983; Green et al. 1985; Green and Penning-Rowsell 1986). These matters remain to be studied more systematically, but we now know that they are of key importance.

At the same time the assessment of the Aldeburgh sea-defence scheme was innovative (Turner, Bateman and Brooke, this volume) in showing the way towards valuing some aspects of environmental benefits, using the ESA payment approach, and an assessment of the recreational gains from maintaining the current beach configuration. Also controversial, the Fairlight Cove coast-protection scheme showed the problematic nature of assessing the benefits of preventing houses being lost to the sea as a result of cliff erosion (Anon. 1988).

Our research between 1986 and 1991 focused on four benefit

categories. The first, and most important in the first instance, is the benefits of retaining or enhancing beach recreation in locations where the beach is used as the engineered scheme for protecting the area landwards. We have undertaken a number of studies (Penning-Rowsell et al. 1989; Coker et al. 1989) which show these benefits to be substantial in cases where there is a population of recreators to be served and where they can be shown to be willing to pay for the maintenance of the status quo or for beach improvements.

Second, we have researched the extra benefits that arise from sea flooding as opposed to fresh water flooding, building on earlier work in the same vein (Penning-Rowsell and Chatterton 1977; Penning-Rowsell 1978). A third strand of the research has been to improve the methods for assessing the benefits of losing property to the sea as a result of flooding (Thompson et al. 1987).

The fourth element in our research has shown – broadly – that the circumstances in which major investment in coast protection can be justified by losing property to the sea are few and far between. This reinforces the key conclusion from this research that in future the rationale and justification for many coast-protection schemes will be the maintenance of recreational beaches and the protection of sites with environmental value. That conclusion can also be applied to sea-defence schemes, where those schemes protect sites from flooding and flood damage which are valued for their aesthetic, archaeological or nature conservation values.

The conclusion must be that the easy approaches to justifying such schemes – in terms of direct and indirect flood damage avoided, and the protection of tangible assets from erosion – will not, in general, yield the kind of benefit sums that will justify major works. Yet major works will often be necessary to maintain even the status quo and the environmental value that the coast currently holds for many people and innumerable wildlife species.

Key questions

The whole subject of the evaluation and valuation of environmental resources raises many questions of a moral, methodological and a technical character. Alan Holland and Jeremy Roxbee Cox (Chapter 2) raise the question of the many different meanings of value: values as a right, and values reflecting preferences. Whose preferences should we take, in this respect, and who decides? Who is deemed to be correctly informed?

Colin Green (Chapter 3) raises the more technical and procedural question as to whether techniques can be developed that aid the quantifying of environmental values: 'will it help'? Will these techniques make difficult decisions any easier; will they clarify issues, or merely confuse? If moral and ethical considerations dominate, what can be the answers about particular sites? John Adams (Chapter 4), in contrast, takes a critical look at using benefit-cost analysis in the environmental domain, and finds it wanting. He raises the question as to whether it is not better, anyway, to rely on the political process rather than resort to techniques of spurious appropriateness.

Focusing down on specifics, and taking a particular site, Kerry Turner, Ian Bateman and Jan Brooke (Chapter 5) look at the distributional effects of investment in coast protection and sea-defence works, among other matters: this raises the question, in the Aldeburgh case, whether it is 'right' that certain groups – in this case the boat club and its users – should gain (by having protection for their facilities) at the tax payers expense? Who gains, and who pays, are at the heart of this debate.

At a more technical level, Sylvia Tunstall and Annabel Coker (Chapter 6) look at the methodological and technical questions surrounding the use of questionnaire surveys to determine environmental values, including the questions of sampling and question complexity when using techniques such as Contingent Valuation Methods for appraising environmental gains and losses. Can we be sure that they tell us what we think they tell us? Do they give reliable results? Would they be replicable?

Thereafter both Annabel Coker and Cathy Richards (Chapters 7, 8 and 9) pose questions about how to approach the evaluation of environmental resources and decisions about coastal management in a more systematic way. Can it be done? And what procedures can we use to maintain an open, systematic and accountable process for involving all interested parties in arriving at a 'consensual (e)valuation' of these environmental values?

Many of these questions cannot yet be answered: some will never be answered. We are only at the start of the process of even deciding whether we can be more systematic in our analysis of environmental values, let alone any considerable way down that path. But there are some lessons that can be learnt, and dilemmas refined.

Assessment

Progress can be made, but not without continual self-criticism.

The nation's economic resources are finite and they need to be husbanded. Public-sector investment should therefore be made on the basis of careful appraisal, rather than decisions to fund policies, plans and schemes being based on post-rationalisation of pre-determined designs. This appraisal will necessarily have to weigh environmental gains and losses against monetary costs and benefits. In this, the way that this weighing is done is important, and a systematic, public and rigorous approach is desirable.

And in the same way that economic resources need to be husbanded, and their allocation and use justified, so environmental protection needs justification and should not be based on the protection of everything, or merely the environmental status quo maintained, regardless of thought and evidence. Choices will have to be made and they should be made on the basis of a careful identification, evaluation and valuation of the resources and options available, rather than just on ignorance and the processes of 'messy politics' that has created some of the environmental damage and wasted public money on coastal protection that we have seen in the past.

It is of course a cliché to suggest, therefore, that an inter-disciplinary approach to coastal-zone management is necessary, and that close interaction between the disciplines is a requirement for harmony and wise decisions. Nevertheless, it is correct, cliché though it is, and one of the main achievements of this volume has been to bring together diverse papers from specialists from disparate backgrounds. It is hoped that the 'ecologists' feel that they have been able to contribute to the debate by indicating both what is at issue and the relative usefulness of different decision aids. The 'economists' may now have a clearer view of areas where agreement is possible and of those areas in which they should 'tread with care'.

This venture, then, has resulted in the clarification of issues relating to both the present situation as regards environmental evaluation and site assessment, and to a consensus, at least among those involved, on a better procedure by which to take coastal-management decisions. It has also charted some of the directions of future research.

And, of course, more research *is* needed . . .

References

Anon (1988) *Fairlight Cove: Benefit-cost analysis*, Fairlight, Sussex: Fairlight Cove Preservation Association (available through Middlesex Polytechnic Flood Hazard Research Centre).

Coker, A.M., Thompson, P.M., Smith, D.I. and Penning-Rowsell, E.C. (1989) *The impact of climate change on coastal zone management in Britain: a preliminary analysis*, Conference on Water and Climate, World Meteorological Organisation, Volume 2, 148-60, Helsinki, Finland: World Meteorological Organisation.

Department of the Environment (1984) *Notes of guidance in the preparation of CBA for works proposed under the Coast Protection Act 1949*, London: Department of the Environment.

Green, C.H., Emery, P.J., Penning-Rowsell, E.C. and Parker, D.J. (1985) *The health effects of flooding: a survey at Uphill, Avon*, Enfield, London: Middlesex Polytechnic Flood Hazard Research Centre.

Green, C.H. and Penning-Rowsell, E.C. (1986) 'Evaluating the intangible benefits and costs of a flood alleviation proposal', *Journal of the Institution of Water Engineers and Scientists* 40(3), 229–48.

Parker, D.J., Green, C.H. and Penning-Rowsell, E.C. (1983) *Swaleclife coast protection scheme: evaluation of potential benefits*, Enfield, London: Middlesex Polytechnic Flood Hazard Research Centre.

Parker, D.J. and Penning-Rowsell, E.C. (1982) 'Flood risk in the urban environment', *Geography and the Urban Environment* (eds Herbert, D.H. and Johnston, R.J.), Chichester: John Wiley.

Pearce, D., Markandya, A. and Barbier, E.B. (1989) *Blueprint for a green economy*, London: Earthscan Publications.

Penning-Rowsell E.C. (1978) *The effect of salt contamination on flood damage to residential property*, Enfield, London: Middlesex Polytechnic Flood Hazard Research Centre.

Penning-Rowsell, E.C. and Chatterton, J.B. (1977) *The benefits of flood alleviation: a manual of assessment techniques*, Aldershot: Gower Technical Press.

Penning-Rowsell, E.C., Coker, A.M., N'Jai, A., Parker, D.J. and Tunstall, S. (1989) 'Scheme worthwhileness', *Coastal Management* 227–41. London: Thomas Telford.

Penning-Rowsell, E.C. and Parker, D.J. (1987) 'The indirect effects of floods and benefits of flood alleviation: evaluating the Chesil sea defence scheme', *Applied Geography* 7, 263–88.

Thompson, P.M., Penning-Rowsell, E.C., Parker, D.J. and Hill, M.I. (1987) *Interim guidelines for the economic evaluation of coast protection and sea defence schemes*, Enfield, London: Middlesex Polytechnic Flood Hazard Research Centre.

2 The valuing of environmental goods: a modest proposal

Alan Holland and Jeremy Roxbee Cox

Introduction

As the authors of the 'Pearce Report' (Pearce et al. 1989) wryly observe, the reckoning of environmental value in pounds and pence 'offends some conservationists'. Perhaps this is because, like William Morris, the conservationists in question have visions of the human experiment all coming to an end 'in a counting house on the top of a cinder-heap' (Morris 1894).

In the account of an interview with David Pearce following the publication of the Report (the *Independent* 1989) it is suggested that the specific cause for offence lies in the fact that attaching a monetary value to the environment 'implies that nature can only be seen in terms of its use to mankind'. The suggestion is that the placing of a monetary value on environmental goods implies a particular philosophical theory of value. This philosophical theory of value is succinctly stated in the Pearce Report itself as the view that: 'Values are . . . entities that reflect people's preferences' (Pearce et al. 1989).

We shall refer to this view, for convenience, as the 'Pearcean philosophy of value'. A notable feature of this view, for our purposes, is that it would appear to be inconsistent with the view held by many conservationists and others, that environmental phenomena have value in their own right and independently of human preferences.[1]

Although a generalised version of the Pearcean philosophy of value has respectable philosophical antecedents and distinguished contemporary advocates,[2] we shall nevertheless contend, in the first part of our chapter (Sections I and II), that it is inadequate even as an account of the value we attach to human beings. Conversely, a theory of value which does explain the value we attach to human beings as such is likely, we suggest, at least to leave room for, or even to encourage, the view that environmental phenomena have value in their own right. We briefly review some alternative theories of ecological value in Section III. Finally, in Section IV, we argue that, even if we abandon the Pearcean philosophy of value, it nevertheless does not follow that we have to abandon the attempt to value the environment in monetary terms. All that is required is a simple adjustment in our conception of the relation between value and human preferences. We end with some suggestions about how this simple adjustment might affect the way in which economists approach the task of assigning monetary values to environmental goods.

I. The Pearcean philosophy of value

Philosophers, like everybody else, find the notion of assigning value to the environment or to ecological phenomena a difficult one. The difficulty is that, at first sight, the environment as such or in its own right does not seem to be the kind of thing that can be declared good or bad. Rain, to take an example, can be good for the farmer and bad for the holidaymaker. But it is quite unclear what we might mean by declaring rain *in itself* to be good or bad. Moreover, even if we do seem to glimpse some notion of environmental value, some sense in which the environment as such is good, we may be unable to glimpse any corresponding notion of environmental *dis*value. Are there environmental ills (things bad in themselves) as well as environmental goods? And can the one notion have a sense if the other does not?

It is quite otherwise when we turn to consider the subjective states of 'sentient' beings (human beings, that is to say, and no doubt many other animals as well). Pleasures, some of them at any rate, are good: feelings of achievement and states of satisfaction are good; most pains, feelings of frustration and states of dissatisfaction are bad. In short, we are comfortable with the idea of good, or bad, experiences, and are happy to regard such items as having positive or negative value in their own right. Accordingly, and assuming that 'sentience' denotes, roughly, the capacity to have experiences, we find no difficulty in attributing value to the experiences of sentient beings; and we therefore hold that such things matter, are important, should be taken into account, maintained, fostered, cherished, and so forth.

But apart from the experiences of sentient beings which are thought to have value in their own right, we also recognise that there are many other things, including many environmental features and phenomena, which contribute to, or are a means to, the valuable experiences of sentient beings. The song of the skylark enhances our morning walk, the mountain stream refreshes us. The stream has what is usually called *instrumental* value. Since we do not make use of the skylark's song in the same way, we may mark the distinction by saying that it has derivative value: its value derives from the contribution it makes to our enjoyment of the walk.[3]

Many philosophers regard the account of value so far sketched as virtually complete and take any assignment of value outside these parameters, such as the assigning of value to the environment as such, to be problematic. Moreover, a reasonably close reading of the Pearce Report suggests that its authors, too, subscribe to some such theory of value, even to a very narrow version of it restricted to human beings. 'Values,' they say, 'are taken to be entities that reflect people's preferences', and we interpret them to be saying that values are *nothing but* reflections of people's preferences. This may not be immediately apparent in view of their recognition of what they term 'existence value' (as identified by Krutilla (1967)) and the contrast which they draw between this and 'user value' (Pearce et al. 1989). Existence value is the value that people may place on the mere existence or continued existence of some feature of their environment regardless of any actual or potential use they may make of it. Many people, the authors suggest, value the remaining stocks of blue, humpback and fin whales in this way. So far, this might indicate a recognition that whales have value in their own right. But such an impression is quickly dispelled when the authors of the Report mention, but immediately set aside, any notion of value that is 'unrelated to human beings altogether'. The existence value of whales, they make it clear, is the value of the existence of whales for *humans*. Putting this together with the thesis that values are reflections of people's preferences, we reach the conclusion that, for the authors of the Pearce Report, the existence value of whales is constituted wholly by the satisfaction that the existence of whales affords of the preferences of those people (present and future) who want whales to continue to exist. Whales, therefore, have derivative value, and the philosophy of value being espoused is a version of the one that we have outlined.

It should be noticed how the reduction of all value to the preferences of people so conveniently facilitates the project of accounting for environmental value in monetary terms. No-one who accepts *that* philosophy of value can ultimately have any objection to putting cash values on environmental goods because, crudely, money is nothing but a measure of people's preferences. (This is not to say that such a cashing-out of environmental goods is straightforward. As John Adams (1990) points out in his review of the Pearce Report, and as its authors themselves admit (Pearce et al. 1989), there can be considerable discrepancies between what people appear willing to pay for the preservation of some environmental good and what they are willing to accept as compensating for its loss, and hence a corresponding uncertainty over the cash value to be assigned.) The question to which we shall return in Section IV of this chapter is whether the project of accounting for environmental value in monetary terms actually *requires* the adoption of the Pearcean philosophy of value.

And this is important in view of the matter to which we now turn, which is the question of the tenability of that philosophy of value.

II. Critique of the Pearcean philosophy of value

It is proposed, on the Pearcean philosophy of value, that the only items in the whole world which have value in their own right are the experiences of sentient beings. But now a question arises about the sentient beings themselves, the people and the animals, that have these valuable experiences: where do *they* enter into the reckoning up of value? For we do as a matter of fact seem to regard people as having value in their own right; and it would surely be odd, or so commonsense seems to suggest, if a person's experiences were valuable whilst the 'owner' or subject of those experiences had no value.

The most immediate response open to the advocate of the position under discussion is to say that human beings as such have *instrumental* or *derivative* value. Our value lies in the contribution we make to the valuable experiences of others or in the use that they make of us. But this response simply fails to do justice to the phenomena. We may indeed have these kinds of value, but they are not the only kind of value that we have.

A second response is to say that human beings have value purely as the possessors or repositories of good or bad experiences. Because these experiences are good, or bad, and thus have value, the person having them has value also. From this point of view, the reason for promoting people's welfare will be that it brings into existence something good – good experiences. Thus, on this view, in order to give a satisfactory explanation of why we have to take account of people's interests, it is not necessary to suppose that anything other than experiences has value. If we accept that experiences are good or bad, we have reasons to think it wrong to cause people suffering, right to further their happiness, etc.; and thus we have reason to take into account people's interests. We are committed to treating people as mattering: without having to suppose that people are of value in themselves.[4] (A preliminary caution: does this line of argument show that on the experience approach we would treat people as mattering, or only that we would treat people *as if* they mattered, i.e. in the same way as we would if we thought they mattered?)

This response does not require us to deny that people have value in their own right, but it does question whether this (possibly obscure) supposition is necessary, in view of the resources of a philosophy of value based upon the relatively unproblematic notion of a valuable experience.

A first comment on this response is to wonder whether it does not precisely have intuitions reversed. For one is tempted to protest that the only reason why experiences have value, are important, or matter, is that they are happening to or are experienced by beings who matter. If the beings who have the experiences do not matter, then why should it matter what their experiences are like?

A more powerful consideration is this. There is a distinction to be drawn between two kinds of thing we may have in mind when we say that something has value, i.e. that it matters, cannot be disregarded, and so forth. On the one hand, when we say that someone has undergone some bad experience, such as severe suffering, we contrast it with other experiences, such as the relief of suffering, which will be good. It matters for someone whether the experience they undergo is good or bad. When, on the other hand, we say that a human being has value, that they matter, we are *not* saying that they are a good thing, to be contrasted with some opposing bad thing. The alternative to a thing's being of value or mattering in this case is its being something of no importance, something that does not matter. (Thus if you carelessly destroy the paper dart I have absent-mindedly made during our discussion, I may truthfully claim that it is not something that matters, it is something of no value.) When, therefore, we claim that experiences have value, we are making a claim of the first kind. When we say that human beings have value, we are making a claim of the second kind. These claims do not compete; they are complementary. But they *are* different. A being with a capacity for valuable experiences matters, has value; but it is not the occurrence of the valuable experiences that constitutes the value of the being that has them.

A further point to emerge from this consideration is the symmetry between the kind of value we readily attach to human beings and the supposedly problematic case of environmental value. In both cases we appear to have in mind that kind of value or importance which contrasts with *un*importance or mere lack of value.

The attempt may still be made, however, to interpose an asymmetry here. The moral philosopher R.M. Hare (1987) has argued that human beings have value in that they value themselves: that is, inasmuch as each human being has value to or for themselves.[5] The same cannot be said of any environmental feature or phenomenon such as, say, a Site of Special Scientific Interest. But, first, this distinguishing feature of humans does not show that they exemplify a different kind of value, but only that they alone are capable of recognising the value that they have. Second, it is hard to see how the reason adduced actually shows that human beings have value. If we each value ourselves, how does this show that each of us really does matter? People can be wrong about whether things matter; perhaps they are wrong about themselves. And if we each value ourselves, how does this show that human beings *in general* matter? It is not even premised that we each value each other. And, finally, there is quite simply a gap between the claim that a human being is valued, whether by themselves or by some other, and the claim that they have value in their own right. The first claim fails to justify the second.

Thus there appear to be good reasons for accepting the symmetry mentioned above. The value we attach to ecological phenomena is of the same kind as the value that we attach to human beings, and the problem of explaining its nature is no greater in the one case than in the other.

III. Alternative theories

If the theory which locates value in the experiences of sentient beings fails to do justice to the value we attach to human beings, it is unclear why we should accept it as providing an adequate theory of ecological value. The problem is not simply that it may give a wrong account of such value. The problem also is that exclusive attention to the interests of sentient beings, and of human beings in particular, may leave many important values unaccounted for. Conversely, it may be that some sentient interests deserve to be *discounted* – the pleasure derived by vandals from the destruction of a tree, for example.

It is not enough, however, simply to dispute the theory that locates value in the experiences of sentient beings; we need to give some indication of what the alternatives are. We do not pretend that a notion of ecological value, as something which is independent of the experiences of sentient beings, is an easy one to defend, and we do not attempt such a defence here. But part of the point of our discussion of the question of the value of human beings has been to show that the problem of ecological value is not a special case, but is in fact one instance of a more general and more fundamental problem in the theory of value.

Perhaps the most favoured alternative, among philosophers at any rate, is the view that locates value in all living things, and not just in sentient beings.[6] The basis for this position is the observation that any living thing has a pattern of development in terms of which it may either flourish or fail to flourish. There is a way-that-it-is-good (or bad)-for-a-living-thing-to-be. Living things can aspire to health; or alternatively can fall ill or be injured. (Plants get 'sick'.) Only organisms such as the smallpox virus itself may be exempt from such generalisations, although even this can die or be killed. The contrast here is with pieces of the environment such as a rock. There is no way-that-it-is-better-for-a-rock-to-be, except for some human or animal interest in its being this way or that.

On this basis, plants as well as animals, but not inanimate things, are assigned a value which is neither derivative nor instrumental and is supposed to be independent of the interests of any sentient being. Just as the good or bad experiences of sentient beings do not *constitute* the value of those beings – or so we have argued – so the good or bad states of living things do not constitute the value of those things. But just as the capacity for good or bad experiences is part of the basis for the ascription of value to sentient beings, so is the susceptibility to good or bad states part of the basis for the ascription of value to living things.

Some philosophers would go further and assign value in some shape or form even to inanimate nature. This may be done in three ways.

First there is the suggestion that value attaches directly to portions or features of nature, such as a shingle bank or river, by very virtue of their uninhibited natural state. The American philosopher John Rodman (1977) speaks eloquently in this vein of a wild river being repressed by the man-made dam which bestrides it, and of its need to be liberated. Were he a native of East Anglia he might have spoken also of the sedate march of the shingle banks down the coast of that region, except where they are hindered by groynes and other human edifices. The Scottish philosopher Andrew Brennan (1984) expresses a similar view when he draws attention to the 'lack of intrinsic function' which characterises natural things and which we have some, albeit slender, reason to respect.

What this suggestion has in common with the previous one is that the basis proposed for the assigning of value in each case overlaps in some measure with elements of the basis upon which we assign value to human beings – their autonomy and their capacity to flourish, showing once more the parallel between the two issues.

A second way of assigning value to inanimate nature is to see it as part of a living organism, like the 'dead' wood within a tree's trunk.

This living organism (Gaia, perhaps (Lovelock 1979)) is assigned a value in turn on the kinds of ground already mentioned as appropriate for living things.

Finally there is the suggestion that the value of inanimate nature, or features of nature, rests on their supporting role in ecosystems (where would the limpet be without its rock?) or on their 'architectural' role in nature as a whole, whether as constitutive of living things (in the form of a species) or as 'containing' living things (in the form of an ecosystem, site or habitat). The point is that whereas rocks, species and ecosystems are not, as such, living entities, they are, nevertheless, too intimately involved in the existence of living things to be thought of as playing a merely instrumental role. The American philosopher Holmes Rolston III (1987, 1988) is the leading exponent of this view, and he has developed a notion of what he terms the 'systemic value' of ecosystems, which highlights their close-coupled relation with living forms and the role they play as the framework which nurtures and is the very precondition of the diversity and individuality found among living things.

These, then, are some of the options available if one rejects the theory that locates value solely in the experiences of sentient beings. While it has not been our object to adjudicate between these options, our argument has been that one cannot refuse to take them seriously if one is prepared to take seriously the view that human beings have value in their own right.

IV. A modest proposal

We have now prepared the ground for our modest proposal. Does the reckoning of environmental value in pounds and pence commit us to the view that values are entities that reflect people's preferences? We wish to argue that the use of monetary values does not have to be rejected along with the Pearcean philosophy of value.

This possibility is prompted by the thought that it may not be the introduction of monetary values as such which is the real basis of the objection to the Pearce position, but, rather, the exclusive attention to human preferences on which its introduction rests. If it is grotesque to ask how much it would be worth for a badger's sett to be left undisturbed, this is in large part because it is grotesque to suppose that what is bad about the sett's being disturbed is the disappointment this would occasion to humans rather than the disappointment it would occasion to the badger.

The project of assigning cash values to environmental features based on the ascertaining of people's preferences is arguably essential both for the execution of public policy and for the protection of the environment. We suggest that this project can be retained even if the Pearcean approach to value is rejected. For the two things are detachable. Quite simply the proposal is *to replace the view that values reflect preferences with the view that preferences reflect values.* That is to say, the preferences are no longer to be construed as what *constitute* the environmental values; rather, they are to be construed as *surrogates* for, or *indicators* of, some independently existing value. The cash value of leaving the badger's sett undisturbed, on this account, would still be a function of the measure of concern expressed by people; but now this concern would be construed as something akin to a thermometer reading – doubtless requiring elaborate and sophisticated devices for securing 'accurate' readings.

Would this merely amount to a distinction without a difference? We suggest not.

To illustrate some possible applications of our proposal, consider this passage from a recent evaluative case study, where the authors refer to the 'option value' approach, which involves ascertaining potential preferences:

> The 'option' value approach reflects that people may be willing to pay to keep this environmental complex as it is now, even if they have not previously visited the area and have no current plan to visit the area in the future. Thus, an identified population is questioned about their willingness to pay for such an option, and from these responses, monetary estimates of the 'economic' value of protecting the current environmental conditions may be derived.
>
> (Parker and Thompson 1988)

The authors do not say how these estimates are to be arrived at. If the willingness to pay of each individual is aggregated, then it would seem either that preferences as such are being given priority, and are being thought of as constituting the value, or at least that the preferences of each individual are being counted as corresponding to distinct valuable entities. But if the willingness to pay were merely averaged, this would show rather that the preferences were being used as a test or indicator of value. Thus, to take an extreme case, a site visited (and only likely to be visited) by two people a year might come out as equivalent in value to one which was visited by 20,000.

This latter way of construing the significance of the expressed preferences will be consistent with assuming that the valuers are revealing how much they find something to be worth, their estimate of a value they think to belong to the site. This procedure is like the one we adopt if we have a precious stone valued by a number of experts. They may not agree precisely on its value, but if their assessments are not too far apart, we will think it reasonable to take the average of the values they report as being a good approximation to the thing's value. The procedure of multiplying their valuations by the number of valuers would give a result that had no significance. We may contrast with the case of valuing a precious stone a situation where it *would* appear relevant to multiply the values revealed by those valuing something. Such a situation would be one where the respondents were indicating how much they enjoyed something and where we were seeking to maximize the enjoyment that could be received by the population they made up. The Pearcean approach implausibly assimilates all inquiries about the values of things to the latter kind of case.

Further, if we take the preference to reflect in this way the value the respondents discern the thing to have, the question of what population is the one to question takes on a new significance. On the standard economists' approach we are seeking to find the benefits to be derived from a certain site, and must therefore identify the population that will be affected, favourably or adversely. However, if what we are seeking to discover is the value of the site, regarded as a value that it has independently of human interests, we must find this out from the people who are in a position to recognise such values. The number of such people is not significant. There is of course still a problem about who these people actually are – the problem of identifying those who are well-informed, those of whom it is reasonable to think that their expressed preferences are reliable indicators of the value that the environmental phenomena actually have. For those who believe that preferences *constitute* value, the trivial, mawkish and sentimental preferences will count along with the best. But if we are seeking the expression of *informed* preferences, then there is a clear role for the ecologist and others who will provide the information that will render the preferences informed.

An implication of this alternative approach may be noticed, for the view is sometimes expressed that where two sites would, other things being equal, be judged to have the same ecological value, the one near a large centre of population will have the greater value. It is obvious how, on the Pearcean approach to existence value, this would be so, and equally clear that on the alternative approach we are recommending, facts about the neighbouring population (if any) will be irrelevant. It is not that the one site necessarily has more value; it is simply that the features that give it the value it has are more accessible.

The approach that we are recommending also has implications for the familiar puzzle about whether to take willingness to pay or willingness to accept compensation as the relevant indicator of the value of a site, in the case of existence values, where no benefit will accrue to be enjoyed by the valuers. Willingness to pay will indicate how much a person thinks the site (or a feature of the site) is worth, compared with other things they might pay for that do not bring him or her any personal benefit – such as famine relief. (Clearly there are many problems to be solved before the expressed or manifested willingness to pay of people in different circumstances can be treated as comparable.) Willingness to accept compensation, on the other hand, will not have any relevance here. If you would pay £100 to save 100 people from famine, but for some reason this is not practicable, it does not follow that there will be some sum, £100 or more, or less, that will compensate you for the failure to relieve their suffering. Similarly, while you might be willing to pay to preserve an environmental feature, it will not follow from this that if it cannot be preserved there is some appropriate sum of compensation that will make up for it to you. Just as it is not you but the hungry who have suffered, so it is the environment that has been damaged, not you. The situation is not one where compensation is relevant.[7]

Conclusion

Our strategy has been to argue that one cannot refuse to take seriously the view that environmental phenomena have value in their own right and independently of human preferences if one is prepared to take seriously the view that human beings have value in their own right. Many conservationists, indeed, may be happier with this account of environmental value than with the account presupposed in the Pearce Report. At the same time we have argued that the project of accounting for environmental value in monetary terms, undertaken by Pearce and others, can survive, and may even be improved in some ways, by the shift in the underlying philosophy of value which we propose.

Notes

1. We shall speak, for brevity, of environmental (or sometimes ecological) value, intending to cover the environmental value of a site, the value of a feature of a site, the value of an ecosystem, a species, a vegetation type, etc.
2. Thus in his influential book, C.I. Lewis (1946) writes: 'Intrinsic value, which is that for the sake of which all other things are valued, belongs exclusively to occasions of experience as such; and value in objects consists in their

potentiality for contributing goodness to such occasions.' In his paper, 'Meta-physical questions for environmental ethicists', delivered at Lancaster Uni-versity on 4 November 1989, Professor Timothy Sprigge, of Edinburgh, said simply: 'If [a thing] really does not have any experience, it does not matter what happens to it'. At the same meeting this view was endorsed by Professor Raymond Frey: 'Just as evaluations issue from creatures capable of making evaluations, so values issue from creatures capable of valuing.'
3 This does not exclude its also having value in its own right, as constituting part of the skylark's experience.
4. The defensibility of such a view is argued by Robin Attfield (1983).
5. Some implications of this approach are developed at greater length in Attfield and Dell (1989). Our wording of this position differs from that of these writers.
6. Leading exponents of this view include Attfield (1983) and Taylor (1986).
7. The famine examples remind us that preparedness to pay need not reflect expectation of benefit to the person who pays, that the motivation need not be self-interested. The use of the language of 'preferences' by those using ques-tionnaire methods in assessing environmental values may encourage the assumption that the expression of preference corresponds to some benefit the respondents expect for themselves. But this cannot be assumed. (For a criticism of the view that all valuations must be, fundamentally, self-interested, see Routley and Routley (1979).)

References

Adams, J. (1990) 'Unsustainable economics', *International Environmental Affairs* 2.
Attfield, R. (1983) *The Ethics of Environmental Concern*, Oxford: Blackwell.
Attfield, R. and Dell, K. (eds) (1989) *Values, Conflict and the Environment*, Oxford: Ian Ramsey Centre.
Brennan, A. (1984) 'The moral standing of natural objects', *Environmental Ethics* 6.
Hare, R. M. (1987) 'Moral reasoning about the environment', *Journal of Applied Philosophy* 4.
Independent, 18 August 1989.
Krutilla, J. A. (1967) 'Conservation reconsidered', *American Economic Review* 57.
Lewis, C. I. (1946) *An analysis of knowledge and valuation*, La Salle, Illinois: Open Court.
Lovelock, J. (1979) *Gaia: a New Look at the Earth*, Oxford: Oxford University Press.
Morris, W. (1894) 'How I became a socialist', in Briggs, A. (ed.) *William Morris: Selected Writings and Designs*, London: Penguin.
Parker, D. J. and Thompson, P. M. (1988) 'An "extended" economic appraisal of coast protection works: a case study of Hengistbury Head, England', *Ocean and Shoreline Management*, 11 45–72.

Pearce, D., Markandya, A. and Barbier, E. B. (1989) *Blueprint for a Green Economy*, London: Earthscan Publications.

Rodman, J. (1977) 'The liberation of nature?', *Inquiry* 20.

Rolston, H. (1987) 'Duties to eco-systems', in Callicott, J. B. (ed.) *Companion to 'A Sand County Almanac'*, Madison: University of Wisconsin Press.

Rolston, H. (1988) *Environmental Ethics: Duties to and Values in the Natural World*, Philadelphia: Temple University Press.

Routley, R. and Routley, V. (1979) 'Against the inevitability of human chauvinism', in Goodpaster, K. E. and Sayre, K. M. (eds) *Ethics and Problems of the 21st Century*, Notre Dame, Indiana: Notre Dame University Press.

Taylor, P. (1986) *Respect for Nature*, Princeton, New Jersey: Princeton University Press.

2 Commentary

The role of the philosopher is to clarify the value-bases which we, as a society, are using as a basis for our economic valuations. Do the neo-classical axioms that underlie our economic valuations have a descriptive validity and represent the way in which we think decisions on environmental valuation should be taken? In the Pearce report (Pearce, Markandya and Barbier 1989) values are seen to be nothing but reflections of people's preferences. If we accept this, then money values should be acceptable in principle, as representing individuals' preferences concerning the environment. In practice this creates problems when trying to assess environmental values which, in effect, reflect the value society places on the environment, since such social values can be said to represent more than just the sum of all the individual values within society. For example, society may value something as part of its total heritage even though this consideration does not influence the valuations given by its individual members. Similarly, society may hold some things 'in trust' for future generations although individuals in the society do not themselves value those things at the present time. This principle seems more clearly established within our own society in the case of human artifacts such as works of art, than it is when applied to wildlife and natural ecosystems. All this implies that society as a whole can hold values which transcend those of its individual members.

In classical economic theory, society is composed of individuals and social values can be no more than an aggregation of those individual values. Thus society has to decide what rules are to be followed in applying price tags to features of 'intrinsic' value. An important contribution which the philosopher has to make is to remind us that society must decide what is right, before deciding what is efficient.

In general, ecologists seem to agree that what is desirable and acceptable in terms of economic efficiency may not be so in terms of the environment itself, where this is seen to have 'non-negotiable rights'. Consideration of this dimension should therefore be applied as a constraint on decisions made on the basis of economic values. This is because values, in economic terms, are subjective and sacrificial (in the sense that one thing can be given up for another), but *rights* cannot be modified in this way. In terms of wildlife, this could mean that we ought not to be prepared to accept a scheme or development which would damage, for example, a Nature Conservation Review Grade 1 site, or lead to extinction of species. Such a course of action could be seen as morally unacceptable. It should be noted that such a moral statement does not correspond with an 'infinite value' on a cash scale, but rather with the concept of 'beyond value'. It is a statement which society as a whole must decide whether it should accept, however strong the economic arguments to the contrary.

This line of reasoning would lead to the conclusion that if only one person visited a site of wildlife interest compared with 200 to another, then that fact would not necessarily make the first site of any less value. The value of the site would not depend on its value in relation to the numbers of individuals who use it, but to an intrinsic value of the species which live there together with the physical, chemical and biological processes that are part of their existence. This can be thought of as the 'systemic value'.

Currently, economics is seen by many environmentalists to be inadequate in its dealings with wildlife resources (Bowers, 1990) as a result of the differing value-bases of the 'protagonists'. This raises the question of how are limits to be placed on the structure of economic decision-making, and by whom? Should 'informed' preferences be used, and if so, who decides who is 'informed'? In our society politicians are expected to represent the people's preferences, since they are elected to represent the community. However, short-term political thinking is often at odds with the long-term time-scale involved in natural processes, or with concepts such as site irreplaceability. Politicians themselves are not free of conflicts of interest – it may be a government department which puts forward proposals for an environmentally damaging scheme which will damage a statutorily designated site.

In the context of a particular development scheme, for example a coast-protection scheme, methods can be developed to obtain monetary valuation from individuals (Chapter 6). Comparisons of the advantages and limitations of two valuation methods – willingness to pay and willingness to accept compensation – raises issues of principle as well as methodological problems. Although willingness to accept compensation for environmental losses initially appears a more realistic measure of individual preferences, responses may include infinitely high values which make a nonsense of attempting to value a site in money terms. Hence willingness to pay is usually considered a more appropriate measure.

To summarise, Allan Holland's argument is that values reflect preferences and preferences reflect values. However, we are still a long way from agreeing whether economic values can adequately reflect people's preferences, or even whether they should. Not everyone would agree that individuals' preferences can be reflected by the assignation of monetary value, with no allowance for non-negotiable rights or moral values. On the one hand, this leads us to a fundamental review of the appropriateness of traditional economic theory to the valuation of environmental good; on the other, it leads to the conclusion that environmental values cannot be reflected adequately by money values.

References

Bowers, J. (1990) *Economics of the environment; the conservationist's response to the Pearce Report*, BANC.
Pearce, D. W., Markandya, A. and Barbier, E. B. (1989) *Blueprint for a green economy*, London: Earthscan Publications.

3 The economic issues raised by valuing environmental goods

C. H. Green

Introduction

I shall approach the question of whether the economic valuation of sites of ecological significance is possible and desirable from the twin tests for all applied research: does it work and does it help? If it is possible, then would it help us as a society to make some difficult decisions? These questions also reveal my bias: my interest in economics is not as a theoretical economist but as a policy analyst for whom economics is only of value if it allows useful conclusions to be drawn.

To trail my conclusions: I think that these are very good questions and, whilst I think we are now reasonably confident that it is possible to value recreational benefits reliably, the position on non-use benefits (the value of an environmental site in addition to any potential use made of that site or the flora and fauna it supports) is not yet clear. Certainly, I consider that the reliable valuation of non-use benefits is more difficult than the Pearce Report might appear to imply (Pearce, Markandya and Barbier 1989), and there are possibly some theoretical problems which require to be resolved first, as well as methodological ones.

To answer the question of whether it will help, I think that economists first need to explore a little more what those who say that some things (e.g. life, wildlife and, indeed, anything that is not available for sale in a market) are 'beyond value' or 'priceless' mean by this statement. The straight economist's answer to this statement is two-fold: any decision involves the sacrifice of one thing in order to gain another, because resources are scarce, and it is the rate at which we choose to make the trade-off that economics terms 'value'. Equally the economist will claim that we do choose even for things which are 'beyond value' or 'priceless' and by doing so we impute values to them. Ergo, the claim that some things are beyond value is falsified.

Second, the economist will note that catatonia, a refusal to choose, is not, however, a viable policy option even for ostriches and faced with a decision as to how much it is worth spending to preserve an archaeological site from erosion, to say that it is beyond value leaves us no further forward. She might try again and ask: does 'beyond value' mean of 'infinite value'? Would you be prepared to sacrifice any number of hospital beds to preserve that one site (scarcity of resources meaning that you have to give up something else that you want in order get that which you want and not something you don't want anyway)? A possible reply is that the objection is to the entire social-political decision-making structure in relationship to the environment. The economist is likely to accept that such an objection renders participation in the current exercise an irrelevance but would be likely to insist that in the desired society resources would still be scarce and choices would have to be made.

Alternatively, the point at issue may be the nature of the decision process itself: a belief that such decisions should be taken by some other process.

However, at times it seems merely like a misunderstanding of economics: an equation of economists with accountants. It is easy to fall into the trap of setting up a straw man of economics to attack. Psychologists and sociologists, for example, frequently set up such easy targets, treating economics as if it was about money. To avoid such a straw man, Appendix 1 (see page 52) is a very elementary description of the basic economic view of the world. Attacks on such straw men also so obscure the target that the key assumptions of economics are not recognised and are not therefore properly debated and tested. Some of the key assumptions in and limitations of economics are listed in Table 3.1.

All fields of knowledge, and hence all disciplines, are in a constant state of becoming; at any point in time, they are mixtures of partial knowledge, contradictory partial theories and hypotheses which will turn out eventually to be false.

It has been said, for example, that a physicist is someone who, on Mondays, Wednesdays and Fridays, believes in the Theory of Relativity and on Tuesdays, Thursdays and Saturdays in Quantum Theory; and who, on Sundays, prays to her god that someone will find a way of reconciling the two: preferably her. Economics is equally in such

Table 3.1   Boundaries of economics

Key assumptions in economics:

- all values are subjective and determined and exist in the mind of the individual
- goods exist in measurable quantities and are not wholly unique
- individuals exist to consume
- values are relative rather than absolute and sacrificial
- we seek to make rational decisions
- rationality is equivalent to consistency with other similar decisions
- society only exists as an aggregation of individuals
- there exists amongst those individuals a degree of consensus in direction if not degree of preference

Boundary of economics:

- economics is concerned with economic efficiency – the maximisation of the value of consumption against the resources required to provide that consumption
- economics cannot conventionally draw conclusions about distributional or equity issues
- issues of morality and justice are logically prior to economics
- economics is a descriptive science: its conclusions only have normative significance if we decide that consistency with other decisions is appropriate to the decision in question
- traditionally, economics has not been an experimental science

Gaps in economics:

- the form of the individual's utility function
- the nature of the motivations underlying individual preference for environmental goods

an unfinished state and so the answer today to the question 'Does it work?' may be anything from 'Yes' through 'In some cases' to 'Theoretically excluded'. It is as futile to criticise economics for what it has not yet become as it is to criticise medicine for not having a cure for the common cold. It is, however, useful to consider what economics should or could become.

The basics of economic analysis

Economics focuses upon choices when resources are scarce. Thus, economics has developed principally around choices between alternatives which compete for limited resources rather than upon choices between alternatives where choosing one would necessarily exclude the other. That is, upon comparisons of alternatives which essentially displace one another rather than destroy one another. Economics typically rephrases the problem of having your cake and eating it as: if you had enough cakes, you could have a cake and eat one; in the meantime, is it preferable to eat it or wait until you have another cake? Thus, when confronted with the issue of building a new road either through a park or through a row of houses, economic analysis does not essentially define this as a choice between *this* road and *that* park or *that* row of houses but between *a* road and *a* park or *a* row of houses *here*. That is, which is the best use of resources at this point in space since whatever is displaced by the road could always be replaced somewhere else.

In looking at choices between actions, economics looks at the changes in the availability of things (or 'goods') in consequence of the choice. The value of an action is evaluated in terms of the sum of the changes in the availability of *things*. The preferred choice is assessed as that which overall leads to the most desirable net gain of changes. In other words, values are attached to things, and actions themselves do not have value other than in terms of their consequences: the ends justify the means, or, rather, any assessment of the desirability of the means, other than in terms of their relative achievement of the ends, is outside of the scope of economics.

This definition of the merit of a means in terms solely of the achievement of the ends is not limited to economic analysis but is also typically true of other forms of project appraisal including statistical decision theory, multi-attribute utility analysis and environmental impact analysis.

In economics, both *values* and *costs* are *relative*, *subjective* and *sacrificial*. Economic values are *subjective* in two senses. First, they are given by the individual: the value of a bottle of scotch, or a day in the countryside, is the value to that individual. Market prices, under some limited conditions, give economists a more or less rigorous method of estimating these individual values. Thus, money values are not the definition of economic values; instead money is only a useful yardstick, or numeraire, with which to compare these values. Money is not intrinsic to economics but merely provides a way of applying it to the analysis of the real world.

Economic values are subjective in a further sense: economic value of a good exists only in so far as it is given by the individual. Whilst other concepts of value exist (Brown 1984; Blomberg 1982; Rolston 1985), these other concepts are not incorporated into economics. Specifically, it is assumed that goods have no inherent or intrinsic value of right through existence. Further, in economics, a society is merely an aggregate of individuals and there is consequently in economics no such thing as a social value: a value given by society as a collective. To repeat the point: the economic model of a society is analogous to a pile of sand; 'society' is merely the collective noun for individuals.

Economic values are not intended to be nor are they absolute values – absolute in the sense of being fixed against some definitive measuring rod. Values are *relative* both because economics is about *choice* and because it is not necessary to know how many times better A is than B in order to choose A over B, only that it is better. In addition, because values are subjective, economists do not generally believe that it is possible to make interpersonal comparisons of value: to compare the enjoyment I get from a glass of scotch to the enjoyment you would get from a glass of scotch.

Values are also *sacrificial*: economic values measure the rate at which we would give up one thing for another. The value of a bottle of scotch, or of a nature reserve, is a measure of the amount of other desirable goods we would sacrifice in order to have the bottle of scotch or nature reserve; or, conversely, what we would require in order to give up the bottle of scotch or nature reserve. Because the individual's choices in the market are assumed to reflect the individual's preferences between goods, money can in these circumstances be used as yardstick to compare the different values of the goods bought and sold in the marketplace.

This use of 'value' is quite clearly different to the use of the term in, for example, psychology (Boulding 1988; Heberlein 1988). Whilst the theoretical integration of values, beliefs, attitudes and behaviour into psychology leaves something to be desired, the presumption in the work of Rokeach (1973), McKechnie (1972) and others is that values are relatively stable (as compared, for instance, to behaviour) and certainly resistant to change; indeed, values are sometimes treated as traits which are part of the individual's personality (Kelly 1955).

As such, psychological values are seen as standards and as rather abstract: unlike attitudes they are not directed at some thing or action. Rokeach (1973) defines a value as: 'an enduring belief that a specific mode of conduct or end-state of existence is personally or socially preferable to an opposite or converse mode of conduct or end state of existence'.

In Personal Construct Theory (Kelly 1955), psychological values are the core beliefs that structure our expectations and interpretations of the world. Events that challenge our understanding of the world are interpreted as being inconsistent with this model and will be seen as very threatening. These core beliefs are overarching across wide ranges of potential behaviours and are absolute rather than relative; they provide yardsticks of the desirability of actions rather than being sacrificial.

Compared to values, behaviour, in the psychological perspective, is relatively ephemeral: a psychologist would not accept that a decision by an individual to cheat on her expenses indicated that she now highly valued dishonesty.

Self-evidently, the economic value I place upon a cup of tea varies not only from context to context (between being in the office and being stranded in the middle of a desert) but also over time within a constant context: sometimes I prefer coffee; at other times, an orange juice and so forth. In psychological terms, nothing very fundamental is going on when I decide to have one rather than the other even though on each occasion I have a clear preference for one rather than another.

Indeed, what are termed in economics 'values' are considered as 'intended behaviours' in psychology and to be situationally specific, reflecting an attitude towards a specific act rather than towards the good itself (Ajzen and Peterson 1988; Tunstall, Green and Lord 1988).

In economics, *costs* are defined as what has to be given up, the opportunity, in order to get those things that are preferred: if you prefer apples to oranges, and have to choose one or the other, then the cost of the apples is the oranges you have to give up in order to have the apples. Costs then depend upon the range of alternatives available.

Finally, economics is epistemologically closer to mathematics than to the physical or social sciences. Like mathematics it is an axiomatic system (Popper 1959); mathematics proceeds by stating a few simple axioms (e.g. 'the shortest distance between any two points is part of a Great Circle') and then proceeds to deduce rigorously a system of conclusions upon the basis of those axioms. As with any axiomatic system, Godel's Theorem sets limits upon the possible development of a system from a starting set of axioms. However, in mathematics, the initial set of axioms is essentially chosen arbitrarily: straight lines may or may not meet at infinity; the shortest distance between any two points may be a straight line or part of a Great Circle. Axioms in mathematics are not intended to correspond to reality; they define instead the properties the mathematical system is intended to have (Stewart 1975). The truth of mathematical axioms is therefore a nonsensical question: when faced with a particular problem, the relevant question is whether the axioms are applicable.

In economics, the use of axioms is closer to the dictionary definition of 'a self-evident proposition, not requiring demonstration, but assented to as soon as stated' (Shorter Oxford English Dictionary). Thus, economics asserts the applicability of its axioms and, if the OED definition is accepted, the truth of the axioms of economics can be tested: if one person rejects one or more axioms, then the axioms fall.

This axiomatic basis is crucial: if we don't accept the axioms (and I will not attempt to address the question of whether or not economics is culturally overdetermined by Western European and North American thought), then neo-classical economics falls. However, the problematique defined by economics as choice under scarcity might well still be appropriate and we could select another set of axioms more to our taste to construct an economic theory to apply to the problem.

In addition to the fundamental axioms, economics has adopted a number of working assumptions for convenience in analysis. These are not axiomatic but are sometimes treated as if they are.

Individuals are assumed to be rational, and rationality in choice is treated as a goal of decision-making. However, in economics, rationality means little more than consistency between choices and preferences. Rationality is used in economics as a somewhat grand synonym for 'consistency'. The OED definition of rationality as 'endowed with reason' might suggest that whereas consistency of outcome under identical conditions might well be a criterion of the outcomes of a rational decision process, it neither defines the process itself nor is it necessarily a sufficient condition of rationality. In measurement theory, the term 'reliability' would probably be used instead of 'rationality' to describe this property. As Simon (1986) notes: 'in economics, rationality is viewed in terms of the choices it produces; in the other social sciences, it is viewed in terms of the processes it employs'. Consistency alone is insufficient as a criterion for rationality since a stopped clock is perfectly consistent without consequently being very useful.

Strictly, for individual choice, economics adds in the missing element tautologically: the individual is presumed to maximise his/her objectives, or self-interest, and his/her objectives are whatever s/he seeks to maximise. For collective choices, an objective to be maximised is deduced: that of a Pareto Optimum.

Thus, consistency in choice is desirable only so long as the objectives are unchanged and previous achievement of the objectives was satisfactory. Economics can only claim to be descriptive, reporting either choices that have been made and past valuation decisions, or those that people say that they would make. However, classically, 'is' does not imply 'ought'. Those values that economics estimates therefore only have prescriptive validity if we agree that it is desirable to be consistent with past behaviour: that what we did yesterday is what we ought to do tomorrow. But it is open to anyone to say that although the public may value this good to this amount, they ought to value it more (or less): that what we did yesterday was wrong and should not, therefore, be used as a guide for future actions (Green and Penning-Rowsell 1986).

Axiomatically, the individual is considered to maximise his/her utility, where utility is defined as that which the individual seeks to maximise. If an individual desires the consumption or availability of a good, then s/he will obtain utility from that good. The individual is assumed to be not only the sole judge of the individual's best interests but also to always make those decisions that are most successful. In considering choices about private goods, essentially those which can be bought and sold on the market, that which the individual is considered to maximise, utility, can conveniently be simplified to selfishness. Moreover, since the individual's behaviour can be observed, and given the axiom of rational behaviour, there is no need in economic theory to inquire why s/he is behaving in a particular way: it is sufficient to observe their behaviour. Indeed, the axiom of rationality may perhaps have been selected in order that economics could proceed upon the observation of behaviour. As Boulding (1988) has observed, there are parallels between economics and classical behaviouralism in psychology.

However, there is a tendency to assume that selfishness exhaustively defines the individual's utility function: to assume that the individual can gain nothing else from the consumption or availability of some good. This is to assume that the individual has no altruistic concerns. This assumption is neither inherent in the axiom of individual rationality nor can it be deduced from it (Sen 1987). To define the individual's utility function as exclusively depending upon selfishness gives the individual the motivations of a sociopath whose behaviour is only constrained by living within an environment of other sociopaths. The casual assumption that selfishness is isomorphic with self-interest led to the expectation that Contingent Valuation Method (CVM) studies would be biased by 'free-riding' (Samuelson 1958).

But, as Margolis (1982) has remarked, in choices concerning private goods, the individual has no way of exhibiting anything else but selfishness: any altruistic concerns which may form part of his/her utility function cannot be exhibited through the choice of private goods. However, when we consider public goods, the individual has the opportunity to exhibit other features of his/her utility function apart from selfishness. Environmental goods are typically public goods. A public good is broadly defined as one whose use by one individual does not deny or diminish its value to another and once provided for one individual is freely available to all. A glass of scotch is a private good since if I drink it, you cannot. A safe beach for swimming, on the other hand, has some of the characteristics of a public good in that if it is safe for one swimmer, all the other swimmers also share in that safety without diminishing the amount of safety available to the first swimmer.

It is also common to make assumptions about the functional form of the utility function itself: how the total utility gained from the

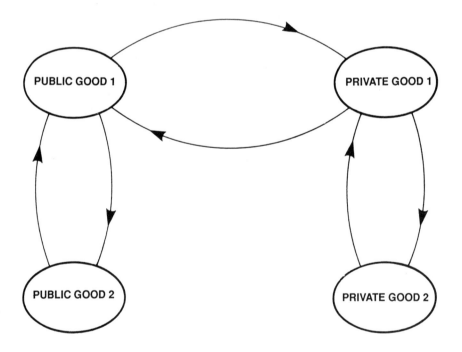

Figure 3.1   Model of trade-offs involved in the provision of a good

availability of some bundle of goods is determined by the amount available of each. Similarly, if an individual gains utility both from selfish and altruistic motives from the availability of some good, then the total utility gained depends upon how these two components are aggregated.

Economics spends half of its time believing in ordinal utilities and the other half in cardinal utilities and the assumptions underlying each model are rather different. For mathematical tractability, rather than any fundamental reason, analyses of cardinal utility typically assume linear, additive utility functions (Green and Wind 1973; Hull, Moore and Thomas 1973). Similarly, Johansson (1987), in an analysis using ordinal utilities, assumes that utility functions are thrice continuously differentiable. Conclusions based upon analyses making such assumptions depend upon the assumptions being true.

Thus, whilst conventional theory (Willig 1976) predicts that the sum an individual is willing to pay for some increase of a good will closely approximate the sum that an individual requires in compensation for an equal decrease in that good, empirical studies show very wide divergences (Banford, Knetsch and Mauser 1979/80; Coursey, Hovis and Schulze 1987; Gregory 1986; Knetsch and Sinden 1984). A number of alternative theories to explain these divergences have been proposed including Prospect Theory (Kahneman and Tversky 1979), Anticipated Utility (Quiggin 1982) and Regret Theory (Loomes and Sugden 1982).

If the possible potential exchanges are summarised (Figure 3.1), then the set in which the divergence between theory and experimental result is least important is exchanges between two private goods. Coursey et al. (1987) have shown that with repeated trials the divergence decreases, and Fisher et al.'s (1988) explanation for initial divergence seems reasonable: we have plenty of practice at buying things but very little at selling them. On the other hand, the respondents may merely have learnt how to play this particular experimental game.

In exchanges between a private good and a public good (for instance, a road scheme which offers reduced traffic noise to local residents but involves the loss of an SSSI), the trade-off can only be assumed to be equivalent to that between two private goods if we assume that the individual has a linear additive utility function. That is, supposing this function has only two elements, self-interest and altruism, that some gain to the self-interest component can exactly balance the loss on the altruism component. However, we know neither the components of the individual's utility function nor its functional form (Green, Tunstall, N'Jai and Rogers 1990b).

Rather than seeking to generalise the choices about public goods on the basis of choices about private goods, it may eventually prove to be that demand for private goods is merely a special and trivial case of a general theory in which demand for public goods is the general case.

Lacking knowledge of the form of the utility function, the practice of asking for willingness to pay rather than willingness to accept compensation merely because the numbers resulting from the latter procedure are 'too large' is hardly acceptable.

Further, in this type of decision, we are asking individuals to make a sacrifice in the 'greater public good'. It may well be that the public do not accept the economic model of society as an aggregate of individuals and the 'greater public good' as being determined by whichever arm of the balancing scale comes down.

In general, the economic worldview of potential exchanges between goods and individuals is typically reflexive and complete: directly or indirectly everything can potentially be sacrificed for anything else. A can be sacrificed for B and so, too, can B for A. Thus, consumption now of A can be sacrificed for consumption in the future of good B by diverting some resources from consumption of A now into investment to yield more B in the future. Or, equally, now or in the future, consumption of B could be sacrificed for future consumption of A. It is only comparatively recently that economics really embodied irreversibility: that some sacrifices once made are irreversible (Arrow and Fisher 1974; Fisher and Krutilla 1978; Henry 1974; Krutilla 1967; Weisbrod 1964). Thus, a fundamental characteristic of time, its irreversibility, is peripheral rather than central to economics. Indeed, economics generally pays little, or no, attention to the dimension of time.

For example, discounting, which is central to benefit-cost analysis (and treats benefits and costs which occur in the future as of lower value than those which occur today), has very little to do with time. Of the two reasons for using a discount rate, one is to reflect the other investment opportunities foregone by making the choice in question: the opportunity cost of capital. That is, the additional consumption that would be generated by alternative investments. The second, social time preference, treats time as essentially a measure of distance: I am presumed to prefer to consume some good now rather than at some point further away in time.

Part of the problem in economics with dealing with time – intergenerational equity being a particular problem, and especially the potential of an intergenerational 'Tragedy of the Commons' (Hardin 1968) – is because society is seen in economics as merely the sum of the individuals of which it is composed, and hence having no continuity in its own right.

In addition, the question of intergenerational equity has tended to conflate the question of whether a project or policy will have a positive or negative effect on subsequent generations together with what weight this generation should put upon future generations' interests. The attempt has then been made to deal with both through the discount rate.

But Markandya and Pearce (1988) point out that lower discount rates will not necessarily lead to the selection of policies, or projects, which are more advantageous to future generations than those which would be selected if higher discount rates were applied. At the same time, the weight that should be given to the interests of future generations is a moral issue and not an economic efficiency issue.

The discount rate is a particularly inappropriate instrument to use to take into account future generations' interests in that discounting applies to consumption whereas the thrust of the intergenerational equity argument is to maintain natural resource capital. Instead, Markandya and Pearce (1988) argue that instead sustainability constraints should be applied: that the trajectory of the project over time should be considered (Green and Tunstall 1991a). Given economics' concern with equilibrium, it is particularly appropriate that a constraint should be applied, that a project should not result in a long-term shift to lower equilibrium than exists at present.

Thus, I would argue in summary that economics may not yet have become that which is required to be applicable to the evaluation of environmental goods: however, we have a choice as to the form of that becoming.

What is not what in economics

A desirable property exhibited by economics is that if something sounds like nonsense then it probably is an economic nonsense. Bad individual cases of analysis do not prove that the analytical technique is fatally flawed: only that not all analysis is well done or that, with more experience, it could be better done.

Adams (1989b) reports that in BCAs of road schemes the value of parks and wildlife sites is taken as the market value of the land in its present restricted use. Further, that the discounted maintenance costs associated with such sites is netted out of this value. In economic terms, the latter procedure is blatantly false.

It is wrong to count maintenance costs of a site as savings associated with a removal of a site since this is to double count by adding both the stock price (land value) and a flow value (maintenance costs). The land price must, by theory, have incorporated into it the discounted value of these maintenance costs.

By analogy, the Department of Transport would wish to consider the risk of a dog being killed on any new road as follows. Supposing your dog is a mongrel which you were given free. Since it has no market value, it would be argued that the economic loss would be zero if it were to be killed. In addition, the argument would go on that since you would be saved the costs of feeding the dog, vets bills, buying leads, toys and so on, there would be a substantial economic gain should your

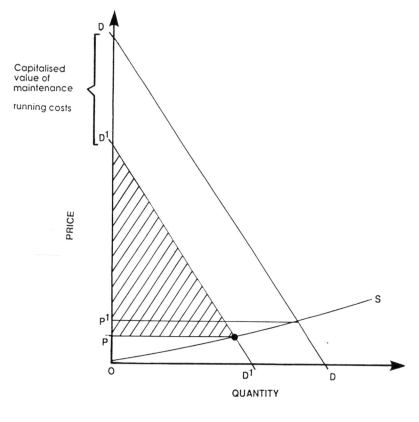

p^1 -- market price if zero maintenance and running costs
p -- market price
D-D   -- demand curve without running costs
D^1-D^1 -- demand curve with running costs
OS   -- supply curve

Figure 3.2   Effect of maintenance costs on capital value of land

dog be killed. New roads should quite clearly in consequence be designed to kill as many mongrels as possible.

This is fundamentally to confuse price and consumer surplus: consumer surplus is the difference between value and price. At the margin, in a perfect competitive market, price equals marginal value. When someone considers buying or acquiring a good, the running or maintenance costs will be taken into account: the effect is to shift the demand curve downwards and to the left (Figure 3.2). In consequence, even if the good is available at a zero price, demand will be less than if the running costs were low.

Similarly, the market price in a competitive market will also be suppressed to reflect the running costs. Since the demand curve has been depressed, the consumer surplus has also been decreased by taking account of the running costs. Therefore, in evaluating parks, wildlife areas or mongrel dogs, it is fundamentally wrong to treat savings in running costs associated with the good as a saving as associated with the loss of the good.

If the market is imperfect so that the market price is artificially depressed or inflated, then the market price will not reflect the marginal value of a unit of the good. Thus the value of agricultural land is less than its market price since the Common Agricultural Policy artificially inflates agricultural land prices. To treat the value of a park or wildlife site as equal to its value in its present use assumes a perfectly competitive market. However, with the presence of planning controls and restrictive covenants, the market is self-evidently imperfect because alternative uses cannot compete for the land. The procedure therefore compounds two questions into one:

(a) should this park or SSSI etc be developed? and
(b) if it is, what is the highest and best use of that land?

Supposing we were to consider redeveloping the Palace of Westminster: it does not have a zero price or value because there is no market for Parliament buildings. The costs of developing it as a park are not therefore zero. Instead, the opportunity costs of its present use equal its value in its highest alternative use: which might be as a hotel, a conference centre or office accommodation. Whatever this highest alternative use might be, it is at least this value in that use which we would forego by converting the site to a park. Further, since we prefer to maintain its present use there is a presumption that the value of the use as a Parliament building at least equals, and possibly exceeds, its value in the highest alternative use.

Similarly, if we are considering building a road over a park, the value of the parkland must at least equal the value of highest use for that land. Since markets are generally imperfect, this will, as in the case of the Palace of Westminster, only give us a lower bound value. In major urban areas, the next best use will probably be for housing or commercial use. Their use for roads is only justified if the benefits gained at least equal their use for these purposes.

The economic value of environmental sites

A wide variety of purposes have been proposed why environmental sites should be preserved (Everett 1979; Helliwell 1973; Reimold, Hardisky and Phillips 1980). Many of these purposes relate to actual (recreation, water purification, monitoring the environment) or potential use (as possible sources of drugs, chemicals or fuel; or as gene pools). Economic valuation of the significance of a site in these terms presents varying degrees of difficulty. Recreational value, for instance, is relatively straightforward to estimate (Tunstall and Coker 1990).

The use value of environmental sites can also of course be substantial (Everett 1977; Farber 1987; Haslam 1973; Maltby 1986). Equally, the use value of some forms of environmental goods can be substantial. It has similarly been pointed out that the introduction of the National Curriculum will substantially enhance the use value of geological SSSIs by generating several million annual visits for educational purposes.

From this economic viewpoint, criteria to assess the significance of a site are the necessary intermediary between the purpose why it is preferable that the site be preserved and the economic value placed upon its preservation. The appropriate criteria which should be used are those that measure the extent to which the particular site contributes to the particular ends, be this environmental monitoring or some other purpose. Thus, in the case of environmental monitoring, a logical criterion to evaluate the significance of the site is the length of record for a site, since the longer the record, the smaller the change in the environment that will be statistically detectable.

For many categories of actual and potential use values, methods exist to provide at least upper or lower bound estimates of the economic value of a site. However, economics also recognises that people may also value the environment for reasons other than the uses to which the environment may be put. Deriving non-use values involves both theoretical and methodological problems.

Non-use benefits

Economics has accepted that the individual, and hence society, may value something for reasons other than the use s/he makes, or may make of it. In seeking to evaluate these non-use benefits, the four technical questions which have to be addressed are:

- what are the goods?
- who benefits, which part of the population so benefit?
- why do they benefit, what motivates their valuation of those goods?
- how do we measure these values reliably?

These issues are discussed in more depth elsewhere (Green and Tunstall 1991a; Green, Tunstall, N'Jai and Rogers 1990b).

What are the goods?

A change in the availability of some goods has no economic consequences unless the individual both has a preference for one level of availability of that goods over another level and can perceive a

Table 3.2   Beliefs about wildlife and geology

	mean	standard deviation
I love seeing butterflies	4.3	0.7
We can never know when a plant might turn out to have important medical uses	4.2	0.8
I would love to see a puffin	3.9	0.9
I would love to see a fossil	3.5	1.2
I miss the flowers and birds of the fields I knew when I was a child	3.4	1.2
The extinction of plants and animals is all part of evolution	2.3	1.3
All rocks look the same to me	2.3	1.2
I wouldn't recognise a fossil if I saw one	2.2	1.2
Birds look pretty much the same to me	2.0	1.0
The plants in gardens and parks are nicer than wild plants	2.0	0.9
Bird watching is like train-spotting: it is only done by over-grown school boys	1.9	1.0
Most insects are pests and wouldn't be missed	1.9	0.9
Plants all look pretty much the same to me	1.8	1.0

standardised item Alpha = 0.77

n = 160

scale: 1 = strongly disagree
5 = strongly agree

change in availability of the goods. If we seek to determine the economic value of improvements to river water quality, we must first determine whether, for example, people's enjoyment of visits to river corridors is sensitive to water quality. Second, we must also determine the basis upon which they perceive or judge the quality of the water (Green, Tunstall and House 1989).

That economic value is given by individual preferences also means that even if a site is judged to have a high ecological value by ecologists, it will have a very low economic value unless that judgement is shared by the public. Indeed, potentially the public might want, and hence be willing to sacrifice other opportunities for, very different sites than ecologists. Similarly, they might prefer to conserve furry mammals whilst attaching no value to, say, fleas.

The results of one survey we undertook suggest the latter point at least is not correct (Table 3.2). Table 3.3, which summarises data from

Table 3.3 Judgements of the relative importance of factors in deciding which nature reserves should be preserved

	mean	standard deviation
It contains wildlife or plants that are disappearing in the UK	4.6	0.7
It includes a very rare species of wildlife or plant	4.3	1.0
It includes a natural landscape rather than a man made landscape	4.1	1.1
The wildlife or plants it contains have always been rare in Britain	4.1	1.0
The variety of wildlife and plants it contains	4.0	0.9
The wildlife and plants it contains are typical of the countryside as it used to be	3.9	1.0
There are no other sites like it locally	3.8	1.2
The reserve contains a large proportion of the plants and animals of that kind in the UK	3.8	1.0
It contains wildlife or plants that are attractive to look at	3.5	1.2
The amount that there is to see when visiting	3.2	1.3
The number of visitors to the site	2.7	1.3

standardised item Alpha = 0.83

n = 160

scale: 0 = least important
         5 = most important

part of the same survey, concerns public preferences as to the importance to be attached to different features in deciding which nature reserves should be preserved. What is of interest here is the relatively low weights attached to visitor features: as in other studies

(Green, Tunstall and House 1989; Green and Tunstall 1991b), the public appear to value environmental sites for what the public perceive as their environmental value rather than for their recreational value.

A further series of problems are created by the need to value some change to some specific site. First, this creates the requirement to predict what effects this change will have upon the ecology of the site and, second, to decide whether or not those effects are desirable.

But, in addition, we do not know whether members of the public attach non-use values to specific sites or a general value to environmental conservation. If we consider just the approximately 5,000 SSSIs in England and Wales, then it seems implausible that the average individual has an identifiable preference, with an associated willingness to pay, for each and every one of those sites. Alternatively, they may have a generalised preference for environmental conservation (Green et al. 1990b). Indeed, that the motivations behind an individual's non-use values include a moral element, as will be discussed in more detail below, suggest that a generalised preference is more likely.

However, choices are about sites: if there is a generalised preference expressed as a willingness to pay, then this must still be translated into the value per site. The sort of decision that must be made is: how much is worth spending to preserve Two-Tree Island in Essex from loss to the sea?

Who benefits?

The population who benefit from the existence of a site cannot be specified a priori (Tunstall et al. 1988). However, since the non-use benefits accruing from a site are the sum of the benefit per individual times the number of individuals who benefit, accurate definition of the population who benefit is as important as accurate measurement of the benefit per individual.

The obvious parameter to explore in order to define the population who benefit is distance from site. One of the purposes of the household interview survey which we have just undertaken was to compare preferences and willingness to pay of populations living from ½ hour to 1½ hours travel time away from the coast (Green and Tunstall 1991a).

Neither the likelihood of stating a willingness to pay nor the amount the individual is willing to pay show any distance dependence. Of seven categories of land use (including houses and bird and nature reserves) for which the respondent was asked to state the priority which should be given to their protection from erosion, preliminary analysis indicates a distance-decay function for: farm land, archaeological and heritage sites, beaches and particularly for promenades. On the other hand, there is very little change over distance in preferences for coastal bird and nature reserves. This implies that bird and nature reserves are valued very much for what they are, rather than where they are, and that the benefiting population should presently be defined as the whole population.

Why do they benefit?

Whilst economists have speculated as to why we value environmental goods other than for their use value, in the absence of empirical evidence these suggestions are no more than hypotheses. If individual valuations for each motivation, including use value, are to be sought through a CVM study then a necessary prerequisite is the specification of an exhaustive and mutually exclusive set of non-use values which have been validated empirically. Similarly, if it is intended to derive a global willingness to pay, the strengths of the different motivations are obvious explanatory variables to use to explain differences in individuals' willingness to pay.

A number of studies (Croke et al. 1984; Green et al. 1987) have reported on the relative importance members of the public attach to different motivations. These studies showed that non-use motivations were typically given greater weight than use related benefits. Moreover, some studies have also indicated that non-use motivations are associated not only with altruistic concerns but also with moral concerns (Green et al. 1989; Green and Tunstall 1991a).

That moral concerns appear to be associated with the non-use motivations raises problems for economic analysis which conventionally seeks to achieve the economic efficiency. If moral concerns are as significant as determinants of non-use motivations, then the problem is redefined towards 'How much can we afford to spend?'.

How do we measure these values?

The only practical way to derive these values is through a CVM study (Cummings et al. 1986). We have stressed elsewhere (Tunstall et al. 1988; Green et al. 1990b) that it is essential that issues of validity and reliability be set at the heart of all CVM studies and that, as yet, each such study must be treated as an experiment (Green et al. 1990a). The outstanding issues described above also imply that technically it is not yet possible to provide well-defined estimates of the non-use values associated with individual sites.

Testing validity requires that the design of the CVM instrument be based upon a theoretical model and we have (Tunstall et al. 1988; Green et al. 1990a) adopted the Fishbein-Ajzen attitude model (Fishbein and Ajzen 1975). In this model (Figure 3.3), willingness to pay is defined as an attitude towards an act.

In the interview survey discussed earlier, the basic theoretical model underlying the design of the interview schedule is that given in Figure 3.4. Willingness to pay for coast protection through increased taxes is predicted to be a function of attitudes towards coast protection (the object of the action) and of attitudes towards the specific payment mechanism adopted (the action). However, willingness to pay is in turn constrained by income.

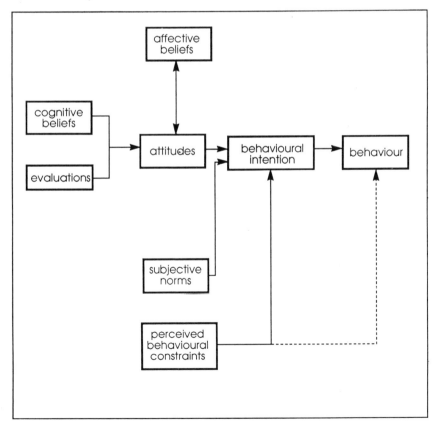

Figure 3.3 Basic attitude theory model

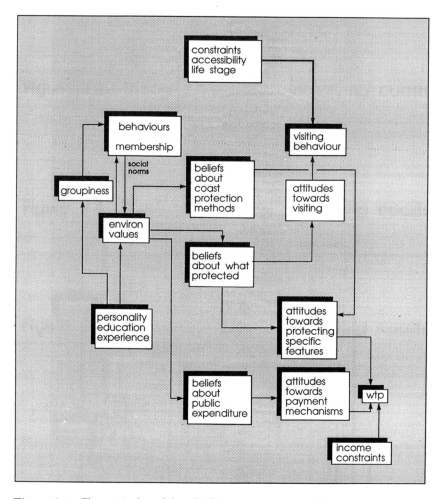

Figure 3.4   Theoretical model underlying coasts remote sites survey

The model being used in the analysis is slightly different; first, the additive model shown has been adjusted to an interactive model for income as discussed below. Second, since some of the statements included as indicators of environmental value orientation are now interpreted as social norms within the context of the Fishbein model, these are being allowed to enter the regression equation as explanatory variables.

A difficulty in operationalising economic theory in the form of a CVM study is to determine what theory means by income: gross income, income net of taxation, disposable income or some other income variable. Theory predicts that willingness to pay for a good should be constrained by income and hence a test of the construct validity of CVM studies is the finding of such a predicted relationship. The results of previous empirical studies have been somewhat mixed and have included negative rather than the predicted positive associations.

As with any failure of construct validity, this may indicate either a failure in measurement or falsification of the underlying theory embedded in the model. In this case, it probably indicates the lack of any clear theory and the need for the researcher to provide sufficient supplementary theory to form the basis of adequate validity testing.

It seems reasonable to suppose that the income constraint which is likely to affect willingness to pay is short-term disposable income. If the household – however a household defines itself – is the basic decision-making unit as to expenditures and purchases, then the relevant income measure is household disposable income. Pope and Jones (1990) use household income divided by the number in that household: since some elements of expenditure are likely to be proportional to household size, this seems reasonable although it would perhaps be subsumed in a measure of disposable income.

However, the functional relationship between willingness to pay and income may well be typically mis-specified. The simplest model which can be applied is:

willingness to pay (WTP) = f(income, preference)

The relationship tested is usually additive:

WTP = income + preference

It is not self-evidently true that this is how we would expect income to act as a constraint since this implies that those who have a higher income will be willing to pay more for a good even if they don't want it. The use of the additive form in this case implies, for example, that a reduction in preference for the good could be exactly counterbalanced by an increase in income; those with low preferences for the goods but high incomes giving the same willingness to pay values as those with strong preferences but low incomes.

A more appropriate model therefore, drawing upon Wheaton's (1985) causal analysis of buffering variables, is likely to be an interactive one:

WTP = income.preference + preference + income

In practice, since both income and willingness to pay are generally highly skewed, it is typically necessary to transform the variables to normality, by the logarithmic transformation, before undertaking regression analysis (Tukey 1977). If this is not done, then there is likely to be a problem with heteroscedasticity (Wetherill et al. 1986); it also has the advantage that if income enters the equation, then the regression coefficient for income will measure income elasticity (Gujarati 1975).

Preliminary analysis indicates that from the model given in Figure 3.4 it is possible to predict with over 90 per cent accuracy which respondents are willing to pay. The proportion of variance in the amounts individuals are willing to pay which can be explained through regression models of acceptable fit according to standard rules (Wetherill et al. 1986) is about 20 per cent. However, further analysis and particularly causal analysis (Joreskog et al. 1979) remains to be undertaken.

Conclusions

I began by two questions: does it help and does it work?

The decision-maker's aim should always be to be able to take slightly better and more informed decisions today than s/he could yesterday. In terms of such a marginal improvement, the first conclusions are:

- non-use values associated with environmental goods are significant.
- motivations associated with non-use components contain a significant moral component.

In relation to the 'does it work?' question, the first and perhaps most important conclusion is:

- it is much more difficult to derive valid and reliable values for use in specific project appraisals than a casual reading of the Pearce Report might suggest (although recreational and amenity benefits are relatively easy to estimate).

Subsidiary conclusions are:

- at present almost all work on the CVM in both the UK and elsewhere is being undertaken as applied research; basic methodological research is having to be undertaken as 'add-ons' to these studies. A basic methodological study is urgently required to ensure that we happen to have hit upon the right instruments.

- it would be unwise to use non-use values for real until such a basic study has been undertaken.
- it would be desirable for researchers in this area to agree a protocol both for undertaking such studies and for reporting them before CVM studies on non-use values are used for real or fielded upon a widespread basis. Demonstration of the validity and reliability of the results obtained will remain a key component of such studies and they are likely remain expensive to undertake for this reason.
- it cannot be asserted that conventional economic theory provides an adequate basis for the evaluation of environmental goods without empirical validation.

Appendix 1 – an economics primer

The basic economic model is illustrated in Figure 3.5. The individual is considered to seek to maximise his/her utility through consumption where utility is a measure of subjective preference. S/he allocates his/her time between leisure (e.g. consumption) and work in order to generate those goods which are not available for free. A good is broadly used to mean anything which the individual believes either contributes to that individual's utility or detracts from it. In other words, values are subjective.

In turn, the production of goods requires a flow of labour (e.g. time) plus some allocation from the existing stocks of land (signifying natural resources) and capital (which includes tools, etc. and which can be thought of as stored time).

It is not necessary to introduce money into this model at all: it adequately describes a simple economy of a one person – two goods economy: a castaway on a desert island who has to decide how much time to invest in climbing trees to collect coconuts and how much time to devote to sunbathing. Investing some time in building a ladder will create capital and increase the efficiency with which coconuts can be collected so that thereafter more time can be spent sunbathing.

If values are relative so too are costs: in economic terms, the cost of something is what you have to give up in order to get it: its opportunity cost. The opportunity cost of using resources in one way, or of consuming a good, depends upon what the alternatives are that could be chosen. A change in the available alternatives may, therefore,

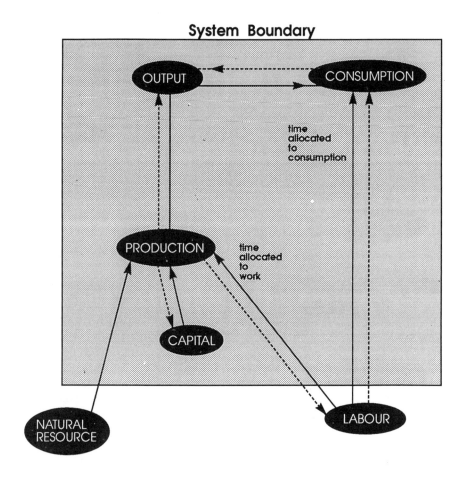

Figure 3.5   Basic economic system

change the opportunity cost associated with the decision.

For example, suppose there are five people with identical preferences: peaches are preferred to pineapples, pineapples to bananas, and bananas to apples. There is a stall with a kilo each of peaches, pineapples and bananas and two kilos of apples. The first five people to arrive at the stall will each be given a kilo of fruit of their choice free of charge. The opportunity cost associated with being fifth in the queue as compared to first is the difference in utility between pineapples and apples; the opportunity cost associated with being fifth rather than fourth in the queue is zero since either way one gets a kilo of apples. The choice then is how long in advance of the stall opening to start queuing.

This example is equivalent to that of queuing outside the Albert Hall for promenade tickets or for the New Year Sale at a department store. One will not queue if there is an ample supply of a desired goods – the value of the goods is not diminished by being in ample supply – or there is nothing on sale that one wants.

Since the individual also has to choose between goods, in the elementary economy, between sunbathing and coconuts, values are also relative and based upon the rate the individual will sacrifice or trade off one good for another. But the value of an additional unit of any good is considered to decrease the more they already have of that good: the marginal utility and value of that good diminishes. This is not necessarily true: to Imelda Marcos, the marginal utility of shoes apparently increased the more she had, or was at least constant.

In more complex economies, with many people and many goods, where no one individual can produce all the goods s/he wishes to consume, individuals have to barter their labour, the use of their capital and goods, in order to maximise their utility in terms of consumption and the time sacrificed for labour. A unit of exchange is generally found rather more convenient than haggling over how many oranges are worth how many eggs: similarly, without a medium of exchange, car companies would have to pay their workers in cars. This unit of exchange then 'lubricates the bartering process' and can be anything which the society chooses. The individual is still deciding how many eggs s/he is willing to exchange or sacrifice for how many oranges: it is merely more convenient to carry out the transaction using the medium of exchange.

So, in a many-actor economy, there is a bartering process superimposed on the basic model (Figure 3.5) and this bartering process is conveniently undertaken using money. The market value of a good is then the rate struck in this bartering process as a result of the different individuals' preferences or values for the good in varying quantities, and the amount other individuals are willing to produce. Since individuals are assumed to optimise their utility, they will be unwilling to pay any more for a unit of a good than its marginal value to them, which depends in turn upon how much of that good they already have.

In such a many-actor economy, an individual's labour could be put to many different uses and to generate goods in different quantities and of different market value. The value of the contribution to output in another use which the individual's labour could generate is the opportunity cost of that individual's labour.

There is similarly an opportunity cost associated with the use of capital: if one person is using a ladder to collect coconuts, another cannot be simultaneously using it to collect oranges. There is also a second opportunity cost: the value of the consumption which was sacrificed in order to generate the capital. In the simple desert island economy, the castaway must sacrifice some sunbathing time in order to build the ladder; in a complex economy, some of the money that could have been spent on consumption is invested instead. Those who seek to invest capital must bargain with those who are willing to sacrifice some of their consumption for the use of that capital.

Obviously, if no one is willing to sacrifice consumption for investment, capital will run out. Equally, capital wears out and must be replaced: ladders do not, for example, last forever. Renewable resources are equivalent to capital in this way; there is a finite stock of non-renewable resources. The different uses of capital will, as will labour, vary in their productivity: the value of goods resulting from that use per unit of capital employed. In the economist's world, resources are always scarce in that there are more things which individually we would like than there are resources to produce them. Clearly, then, as with labour and natural resources, capital should first be allocated to its most productive use and so forth, until the productivity of the next unit of capital invested in production equals the value of the consumption sacrificed.

Under some very restrictive conditions, known as a perfect market, all these allocation decisions can take place through the bargaining of the market place and result in the most efficient solution for everyone. If the different amounts of a good the different individuals in the economy are willing to buy for different prices are aggregated, then the market price struck in the bargaining process will be such that it equals the marginal value of that unit of the good. If the good is thought of as being auctioned one unit at a time where the potential purchasers do not know how much will be sold, then the person who most desires the good will pay a high price for the first unit of the good, equal to his/her marginal value for that unit of the good. The next unit will fetch a slightly lower price either because this is sold to the individual who places the second highest marginal value on that good, or because the first individual places a lower value on the second unit than the first. And so on until no more of the good is available.

However, because it is not generally possible to conceal the amount of goods available, there is a common price for all units of that good. The difference between this common price and what the different individuals would have been willing to pay for each unit of the good sold on the market is the consumer surplus. Equally, in such a perfect market, it can be shown that this price equals the marginal production cost of the last unit of good sold as well as its marginal value: the cost of each additional unit produced tends to rise the more that are produced. Producing any more or less of the good would be inefficient since its cost would respectively either exceed its market value or be below its value. All the allocation decisions in the demand and supply of goods, capital, labour and natural resources occur both optimally and automatically. The system is also homeostatic: it reacts to a disturbance by adjusting to a new equilibrium. In this best possible of all possible worlds, not only is the system self-regulating but it self-corrects to a new optimum.

The Panglossian world of a perfect market is the economic equivalent to the concept of a perfect gas in physics: it does not actually exist but it is a good starting point for analysis. In practice, markets for goods are imperfect in various ways so that prices are distorted away from values, or the good itself may not marketed. In the first case, the market prices have to be corrected, shadow prices inferred, in order to estimate values. For example, agricultural prices in Europe and most of the rest of the world are distorted by the effects of subsidies, price-support schemes or production limits. Where a good is not marketed, then values must be inferred by other means.

Moreover, for the system to be optimal and self-correcting, all goods would have to have prices. If there are some which do not, such as pollution from a factory or traffic noise, then the equilibrium of the system will not be optimal nor will it self-correct for changes.

This simple world has so far assumed both that the individuals in it have an infinite lifespan and ignored the time delays between investing capital and production being yielded as a result. The castaway could choose to plant and nurture some of the coconuts in order to increase the supply of coconuts in future years, sacrificing consumption and time this year for increased consumption in future years. Assuming that the castaway has at least a subsistence diet this year, then the castaway must decide the rate at which s/he is willing to sacrifice consumption now for increased consumption in some years' time.

It is generally assumed in economics that individuals have a time preference for consumption: consumption now of some quantity of goods is preferred to consumption of the same quantity of those goods at some date in the future, all other circumstances being the same. Hence the castaway will not be willing to sacrifice five coconuts for planting if the result will only be an additional five coconuts in the tenth year after planting.

The validity of the assumption of a time preference does not appear to have been tested; instead it is treated as being self-evidently true. The desirability of consumption now rather than at a later point in time is in any case clouded by four other factors:

- variations in the utility of a good over time (I currently place very little utility on a Zimmer frame or in trips to discos).
- decreasing marginal utility of goods (I would certainly prefer the option of £1 million consumption spread out over a number of years to £1 million for consumption – not investment – within a single year). Moreover, if I expect the economy overall to expand, a given increase in the availability of some good in the future is likely to be less desirable than the same increase now because I expect there to be more of that good in the future anyway.
- consumption requires the availability of both the goods and time to consume that goods: offered a holiday in the Seychelles, I prefer to take it in the future when I have time to enjoy it. Equally, I am willing to pay high interest charges using a credit card to buy wallpaper, for example, at times when I have time to decorate my house.
- the elasticity of substitution of capital for income: market imperfections mean that borrowing for investment may be possible only at very high rates.

Million pound football-pools winners who spend all of their winnings in two years do appear to have very pronounced time preferences for consumption. So, too, do small children who want an ice cream now rather than after they have had their dinner.

The actual choice by the castaway would be complicated by considerations of risk (e.g. of partial crop failure); and the need to replace ageing coconut palms as their productivity declined. However, these considerations are additional to the castaway's time preference.

Unfortunately, we do not have an infinite life and hence the gains or losses from decisions we take may only be reaped by our children or future generations. Since we notoriously can't take it with us, the purely selfish but rational individual would aim to expire at the exact moment s/he had no more savings or borrowings to consume. The medieval practice of leaving money to pay for Masses to be said for the repose of the dead can be viewed either as a way of taking your money with you or as a good marketing exercise.

The basic economic model is, however, not readily extendable to other generations because it lacks both a sense of time and because it is composed of individuals. In economics, all men and women are islands. To deal with intergenerational issues, external constraints must be placed upon the basic economic model.

References

Adams, J. G. U. (1989a) *Unsustainable Economics*, London: University College.

Adams, J. G. U. (1989b) *London's Green Spaces: What are They Worth?*, London: London Wildlife Trust/Friends of the Earth.

Ajzen, I. and Peterson, G. L. (1988) Contingent Value Measurement: The Price of Everything and the Value of Nothing, in Peterson, G. L., Driver, B. L. and Gregory, R. (eds) *Amenity Resource Evaluation: Integrating Economics with Other Disciplines*, State College: Venture.

Arrow, K. J. and Fisher, A. C. (1974) Environmental preservation, uncertainty, and irreversibility, *Quarterly Journal of Economics* 88, 312–19.

Banford, N. D., Knetsch, J. L. and Mauser, G. A. (1979/80) Feasibility Judgements and Alternative Measures of Benefits and Costs, *Journal of Business Administration* II, 25–35.

Blomberg, G. D. (1982) Coastal Amenities and Values: Some Pervasive Perceptions Expressed in Literature, *Coastal Zone Management Journal* 10, 1/2, 53–78.

Boulding, K. E. and Lundstedt, S. B. (1988) Value Concepts and Justifications in Peterson, G. L., Driver, B. L. and Gregory, R. (eds) *Amenity Resource Evaluation: Integrating Economics with Other Disciplines*, State College: Venture.

Brookshire, D. S., Eubanks, L. S. and Sorg, C. F. (1986) Existence Values and Normative Economics: Implications for Valuing Water Resources, *Water Resources Research* 22(11), 1509–18.

Brookshire, D. S. and Smith, V. K. (1987) Measuring Recreational Benefits: Conceptual and Empirical Issues, *Water Resources Research* 23(5), 931–5.

Brown, T. C. (1984) The concept of Value in Resource Allocation, *Land Economics* 60(3), 231–46.

Coursey, D. L., Hovis, J. L. and Schulze, W. D. (1987) The disparity between willingness to accept and willingness to pay measures of value, *The Quarterly Journal of Economics*, 679–90.

Croke, K. G., Swartzman, J. D. and Brenniman, G. R. (1984) The relationship between perceived motivation for water pollution abatement programs and preferred methods for financing such programs, *Journal of Environmental Systems* 14(4), 395–404.

Cummings, R. G., Brookshire, D. S. and Schulze, W. D. (1986) *Valuing environmental goods: an assessment of the 'contingent valuation method'*, Totowa: Rowman and Allanheld.

Everett, R. D. (1977) A Method of Investigating the Importance of Wildlife to

58   C. H. Green

Countryside Visitors, *Environmental Conservation* 4(3), 227–31.

Everett, R. D. (1979) The Functions of Wildlife and their Possible Use for Deriving Site Selection Components, *Biological Conservation*, 207–18.

Farber, S. (1987) The Value of Coastal Wetlands for Protection of Property against Hurricane Wind Damage, *Journal of Environmental Economics and Management* 14, 143–51.

Fishbein, M. and Ajzen, I. (1975) *Belief, Attitude, Intention and Behavior*, Reading, Mass: Addison-Wesley.

Fisher, A. C. and Krutilla, J. V. (1978) Resource conservation, environmental preservation, and the rate of discount, *Quarterly Journal of Economics* 139, 358–70.

Fisher, A., McClelland, G. H. and Schulze, W. D. (1988) Measures of Willingness to Pay versus Willingness to Accept: Evidence, Explanations, and Potential Reconciliation, in Peterson, G. L., Driver, B. L. and Gregory, R. (eds) *Amenity Resource Evaluation: Integrating Economics with Other Disciplines*, State College: Venture.

Frank, R. H. (1987) If Homo Economicus Could Choose His Own Utility Function, Would He Want One with a Conscience?, *The American Economic Review*, 593–604.

Goodin, R. E. (1982) Discounting discounting, *Journal of Public Policy* 2(1), 53–72.

Green, C.H. (1990) Oil and Water? Environmental Economics and Ethics, paper given at the First International Conference on Ethics and Environmental Policies, Borca di Cadore.

Green, C. H. and Penning-Rowsell, E. C. (1986) Evaluating the intangible benefits and costs of a flood alleviation proposal, *Journal of the Institution of Water Engineers and Scientists* 40, (3), 229–48.

Green, C. H., Suleman, S. M. and Wood, J. (1987) Investment appraisal for urban storm drainage in Gujer, W. and Krejci, V. (eds) *Proceedings of the 4th International Conference on Urban Storm Drainage*, Lausanne: Ecole Polytechnique.

Green, C. H. and Tunstall, S. M. (1991a) Is the economic evaluation of environmental goods possible? *Journal of Environmental Management*, 33, 123–41.

Green, C. H. and Tunstall, S. M. (1991b) The amenity and environmental value of river corridors in Britain, in Boon, P. J., Calow, P. and Petts, G. E. (eds) *River Conservation and Management*, London: John Wiley & Sons.

Green, C. H., Tunstall, S. M. and House, M. A. (1989) Evaluating the benefits of river water quality improvement, in van der Staal, P. M. and van Vught, F. A. (eds) *Impact Forecasting and Assessment: methods, results, experience*, Delft: Delft University Press.

Green, C. H., Tunstall, S. M., Penning-Rowsell, E. C. and Coker, A. (1990a) *The benefits of coast protection: results from testing the Contingent Valuation Method (CVM) for valuing beach recreation*, paper given at the Conference of the River and Coastal Engineers, Loughborough.

Green, C. H., Tunstall, S. M., N'Jai, A. and Rogers, A. (1990b) The evaluation of environmental goods, *Project Appraisal*, 5(2), 70–82.

Green, P. E. and Wind, Y. (1973) *Multiattribute decisions in marketing: a measurement approach*, Hinsdale: Dryden Press.

Gregory, R. (1986) Interpreting Measures of Economic Loss: Evidence from Contingent Valuation and Experimental Studies, *Journal of Environmental Economics and Management* 13, 325–37.

Gujarati, D. (1975) *Basic Econometrics*, Tokyo: McGraw-Hill Kogakusha.

Hardin, G. (1968) The Tragedy of the Commons, *Science* 162, 1243–48.

Haslam, S. M. (1973) The Management of British Wetlands: 1. Economic and Amenity Use, *Journal of Environmental Management* 1, 303–20.

Haveman, R. H. (1969) The Opportunity Cost of Displaced Private Spending And the Social Discount Rate, *Water Resources Research* 5(5), 947–57.

Heberlein, T. A. (1988) Economics and Social Psychology in Amenity Valuation, in Peterson, G. L., Driver, B. L. and Gregory, R. (eds) *Amenity Resource Evaluation: Integrating Economics with Other Disciplines*, State College: Venture.

Helliwell, D. R. (1973) Priorities and Values in Nature Conservation, *Journal of Environmental Management* 1, 85–127.

Henry, C. (1974) Investment decisions under uncertainty: the irreversibility effect, *American Economic Review* 64,(6), 1006–12.

Hull, J. C., Moore, P. G. and Thomas, H. (1973) Utility and its Measurement, *Journal of the Royal Statistical Society, Series A*, 136(2), 226–47.

Johansson, P-O. (1987) *The economic theory and measurement of environmental benefits*, Cambridge: Cambridge University Press.

Joreskog, K. G., Sorbom, D. and Magidson, J. (1979) *Advances in Factor Analysis and Structural Equation Models*, Lanham: University Press of America.

Kahneman, D. and Tversky, A. (1979) Prospect theory: an analysis of decisions under risk, *Econometrica* 50, 81–109.

Kelly, G. A. (1955) *The Psychology of Personal Constructs*, New York: W. W. Norton.

Knetsch, J. L. and Sinden, J. A. (1984) Willingness to Pay and Compensation Demanded: Experimental Evidence of an Unexpected Disparity in Measures of Value, *Quarterly Journal of Economics* 99, 49–72.

Krutilla, J. A. (1967) Conservation reconsidered, *American Economic Review* 57(4), 77–86.

Lancaster, K. (1974) *Introduction to modern microeconomics*, Chicago: Rand McNally.

Loomes, G. and Sugden, R. (1982) Regret Theory: An Alternative Theory of Rational Choice Under Uncertainty, *The Economic Journal* 92, 805–24.

McKechnie, G. (1972) *The environmental response inventory*, Berkeley: University of California.

Madriaga, B. and McConnell, K. E. (1987) Exploring existence value, *Water Resources Research* 23(5), 936–42.

Maltby, E. (1986) *Waterlogged Wealth*, London: Earthscan.

Margolis, H. (1982) *Selfishness, Altruism and Rationality*, Chicago: Chicago University Press.

Markandya, A. and Pearce, D. W. (1988) *Environmental Considerations and the*

Choice of the Discount Rate in Developing Countries, Washington: World Bank.

Martinez-Alier, J. (1987) *Ecological Economics*, London: Basil Blackwell.

Nash, G. A. (1973) Future generations and the social rate of discount, *Environment and Planning* 5(5), 611–17.

Page, T. (1977) Equitable use of the resource base, *Environment and Planning A*,9, 15–22.

Pearce, D. W. and Markandya, A. (1989) *Environmental Policy, Benefits: Monetary Evaluation*, Paris: OECD.

Pearce, D. W., Markandya, A. and Barbier, E. B. (1989) *Blueprint for a Green Economy*, London: Earthscan.

Pope, C. A. and Jones, J. W. (1990) Value of Wilderness Designation in Utah, *Journal of Environmental Management* 30, 157–74.

Popper, K. R. (1959) *The Logic of Scientific Discovery*, London: Hutchinson.

Quiggin, J. (1982) A Theory of Anticipated Utility, *Journal of Economic Behaviour and Organization* 3, 323–43.

Randall, A. and Stoll, J. R. (1983) Existence value in a total valuation framework, in Rowe, R. D. and Chestnut, L. G. (eds) *Managing Air Quality and Scenic Resources at National Parks and Wilderness Areas*, Boulder: Westview.

Reimold, R. J., Hardisky, M. A. and Phillips, J. H. (1980) Wetland Values – A Non-consumptive Perspective, *Journal of Environmental Management* 11, 77–85.

Rokeach, M. (1973) *The Nature of Human Value*, New York: Free Press.

Rolston, H. (1985) Valuing Wildlife, *Environmental Ethics* 7, 23–48.

Samuelson, P. A. (1958) The pure theory of public expenditure, *Review of Economics and Statistics* 36, 387–89.

Sen, A. (1987) *On Ethics and Economics*, London: Basil Blackwell.

Simon, H. A. (1986) Rationality in Psychology and Economics, in Hogarth, R. M. and Reder, M. W. (eds) *Rational Choice: The Contrast between Economics and Psychology*, Chicago: University of Chicago.

Stewart, I. (1975) *Concepts of Modern Mathematics*, Harmondsworth: Penguin.

Takayama, A. (1982) On Consumer's Surplus, *Economic Letters* 10, 35–42.

Tukey, J. W. (1977) *Exploratory Data Analysis*, Reading, Mass: Addison-Wesley.

Tunstall, S. M. and Coker, A. (1990) *Survey-based valuation methods* in this volume.

Tunstall, S. M., Green, C. H. and Lord, J. (1988) *The Contingent Valuation Method*, Enfield: Flood Hazard Research Centre.

Weisbrod, B. (1964) Collective consumption services of individual consumption goods, *Quarterly Journal of Economics* 78, 471–77.

Wetherill, G. B., Duncombe, P., Kenward, M., Kollerstrom, J., Paul, S. R. and Vowden, B. J. (1986) *Regression Analysis with Applications*, London: Chapman and Hall.

Wheaton, B. (1985) Models for the Stress-Buffering Functions of Coping Resources, *Journal of Health and Social Behavior* 26, 352–64.

Willig, R. D. (1976) Consumer's Surplus Without Apology, *American Economic Review* 66(5), 589–97.

3 Commentary

Site-specific valuations of environmental goods are considered by many to be highly problematic as they raise the moral issue of intergenerational equity. This is comparable with the moral arguments already discussed in the previous section. If intergenerational equity cannot be accommodated in classical economic analysis, it has to be seen as a moral or ethical constraint on the decision-making process. Colin Green's view is that it would be possible for intergenerational equity to be dealt with by the inclusion of a sustainability constraint, in a similar way to that suggested in 'The Pearce Report' (Pearce, Markandya and Barbier 1989).

Another stumbling block when using neo-classical economic theory in cost-benefit analysis is the question of how to handle the discount rate. The present high discount rate (6 per cent) could be amended or even removed altogether, in view of the fact that the value of wildlife to future generations is thereby reduced almost to insignificance. However the 'value' of wildlife does not decline with time, on the contrary, it could be said to increase assuming the total amount available decreases. An alternative view is that if the discount factor represents the social opportunity cost of capital, then it should be retained; but if it is a time-preference model then it should be questioned. Intergenerational equity problems may also arise if all the benefits occur immediately, or on a short time-scale, whereas all the problems and costs are in the future.

Decision-makers and economists in particular need clarification on the subject of specific and relative site values in order to better inform their choices. Although many economists consider it desirable to place a monetary value on environmental goods, ecologists on the whole consider that it is not possible at the present time and within the present economic framework, as insufficient regard is given to the 'real value', i.e. intrinsic worth or non-use value, of wildlife. In view of the reluctance of some ecologists to put a monetary value on any aspect of the environment (McBurney 1990), those needing to value the environment for decision-making purposes, e.g. politicians, may put their own valuation on it. Development decisions have to go ahead, choices have to be made, frequently with inadequate resources and information in several other fields as well as in the environment. Some ecologists believe that it is possible to develop methods by which expression of these values could be given to the ecological importance of a site. However, it might be more important to ensure that ecological considerations are adequately included in decision-making processes rather than concentrating efforts on developing methods for actual monetary valuation.

Given that attempts will be made to put monetary values on the environment, several possibilities already exist for assigning economic values. First, the theory of 'shadow projects'; these are also known as 'planning gains' by which a developer agrees to reproduce a site elsewhere if it is destroyed as a result of development. But 'shadow projects', also known as 'mitigation packages', have a poor reputation with environmental groups. They are seen as 'bribery', the outcome of which is rarely delivered or may be non-deliverable. In theory, this principle could however be used to calculate the cost of the creation of an alternative 'identical' site. In the case of coastal sites these costs would be extremely high as many sites are unique. Thus, if we could value sites in this way, such very high ecological values would dominate the decision-making. This would give ecological sites a similar status to property in British law, with comparable scales of value on prime sites. However, would the Treasury, for example, accept the high levels of value that would be acceptable to an ecologist?

A second approach is to consider the purchase cost of sites for the nation by the State or National Trust. Agricultural land is at present comparatively inexpensive, with many sites of environmental value on low-grade agricultural land in any case. The disadvantage of using land prices as an indicator of value is that there would be no explicit ecological or amenity value, but rather only a reflection of the current market situation at a particular point in time, heavily influenced by agricultural land values. Through the purchase of the land in this way, sites would not be given an ecologically realistic monetary value, even though they would receive a valuation. At present, there does not appear to be the political will to carry out such a policy in a comprehensive fashion, although the National Heritage Memorial Fund, for example, does purchase land for the nation. In doing so, it implicitly recognises certain kinds of ecological value through providing grant aid for such purchases.

Another possible system of valuation is through the use of inheritance tax allowances. At present this method is applied in the case of Areas of Outstanding Natural Beauty (AONBs) where the Inland Revenue defrays inheritance taxes if land is left to the nation or to a recognised organisation, with the owner agreeing to maintain its character and guarantee access during their lifetime. If the land is sold, the new owner must keep to the conditions or become liable for repayment. The approach could also be used to determine the value of Sites of Special Scientific Interest (SSSIs) to the nation.

An opposing view to arguments in favour of monetary valuations is that a high value has already been placed, in principle, on the national series of SSSIs, some 5,000 sites, by a system of government protection, grant aid, compulsory purchase and compensation payments. That this notion of ecological value is only 'in principle' is sometimes shown when a development proposal is made. An example is the recent conflict at Rainham Marshes, where a development scheme worth £250 million was proposed even though the site was an SSSI. Some ecologists would consider that however high the benefits of the development, they cannot compensate for destroying a marshland which will then be gone for ever. From this perspective, government is often seen as not adequately recognising the ecological value of such sites. However, it is necessary to ask whether any method of economic valuation would ever be adequate when weighed against the benefits of development. Perhaps a more fruitful direction for future research, rather than the development and refinement of valuation methods, would be to concentrate effort and resources on improving current approaches to decision-making so that the ecological importance of an area is considered as a constraint on the decision-making process. But benefit-cost analysis will continue to operate as a tool to aid decision-making, at least in the near future, and the monetary valuation of ecological interest will be seen by many as an important part of that tool.

Opinions are often strongly divided on the use of monetary valuation methods for ecological sites. One approach is to pursue a number of methods by which monetary value could be assigned, as outlined above, even if they appear crude and inadequate at present. Another point of view is that the methods for assessing monetary value are inadequate and can easily be based on the wrong premise, for example a so-called ecological value being based on the value of low-cost agricultural land, so that they can lead to inadequate conclusions being drawn and inappropriate decisions being taken.

References

Pearce, D. W., Markandya, A. and Barbier, E. B. (1989) *Blueprint for a Green Economy*, London: Earthscan Publications.
McBurney, S. (1990) *Ecology into economics won't go*, Green Books, Bideford.

4 'Horse and rabbit stew'

John Adams

Introduction

The question posed in this volume is, if it is thought desirable to improve evaluations of gains and losses of environmental goods in economic analysis, then is it possible?

The simple answer is 'yes'. It has been done for grizzly bears in Wyoming, USA (Pearce et al. 1989). Hunters were asked how much they would be prepared to pay for a 90 per cent probability that there would be grizzly bears to hunt in Wyoming in five years' time. The answer was $21.50. Or for a 25 per cent probability in 15 years' time the answer was $8.50. But the hunters would be willing to pay $21.80 for a programme that would ensure a 90 per cent probability of grizzly bears being there to observe in five years' time. The existence value of knowing that the bears are there but not necessarily planning to go to see them – again a 95 per cent probability in five years' time – was $24.00, and $15.20 in 15 years' time.

So such valuation is possible. The question I think is more interesting is does it mean anything? I do not think it does. Indeed it is intriguing to imagine how interviewers get people to play these games, and what goes on in the minds of people being pressed for a cash value in situations like that.

The argument about benefit-cost analysis has been running for some years and it seems to go in cycles. After the Roskill Commission (1971) it went quiet for some time and it has now surfaced again. I find a depressing lack of progress between the arguments that were used 20 years ago, at the time of Roskill, and those that are occurring now, although it does have the benefit of allowing me to reassess 20-year-old material.

Roskill: the arguments revisited

The challenges facing the Roskill Commission 20 years ago were the traffic forecasts up to the late 1960s. These forecasts for London airport gave a sense of urgency to the Roskill exercise in finding a site for the third London airport. I was asked to write a review of the Roskill report for *Area* (Adams 1970) and initially I had volumes of material on the largest benefit-cost analysis in the history of mankind. I had these tremendously exciting computer models for modelling traffic and all these exciting valuation methods.

But in reality Roskill was focusing overwhelmingly on only two things. First, there was the convenience of passengers getting to and from the airport and second the local impacts of the airport. There were voluminous details in the Commission's report on noise-contour lines around the proposed airport and on estimating the valuations of house prices near the airport and of old Norman churches and so on. The projected increase in traffic was some 15-fold; most of this traffic was either starting or ending in London itself. A 15-fold increase in the number of tourists coming to London struck me as being bound to have a dramatic effect on the character of London and this was being wholly ignored. That was the single most important impact of the whole exercise by far, and totally ignored.

That was where I came upon this useful description of benefit-cost analysis as being a recipe for horse and rabbit stew. The recipe is minutely detailed in its description of the preparation of the rabbit. This is the detailed analysis of noise contours, property valuations and tourist numbers, and all the detailed local impacts, airport design and so on. Then, the recipe continues, 'throw in one horse'. It is not surprising that the stew tastes more of horse than of rabbit. Benefit-cost analysis somehow fosters this tendency to concentrate your intellectual energies on the things that can be measured and quantified, especially in cash terms, and shrug your shoulders at the problems that are just too large to embrace.

I came to the conclusion of Hyde Park airport. In order to illustrate what I thought was wrong I invented the inquiry into a fourth London airport in about the year 2006. I did a simple benefit-cost analysis and noted that by then – extrapolating present trends – there would be hundreds and millions of passengers every year. If one could save them all a significant amount of travel time, there would be huge benefits. The closer you get to central London the lower the average access cost will be, and if you save hundreds and millions of people a lot of time in reaching the airport every year you can afford to buy and to demolish lots of buildings to make way for the Hyde Park airport. For example, Roskill valued the old Norman church of Stukely at £50,000 – that is what it was insured for. I asked Westminster Abbey how much they were insured for: the answer was £1.5 million. A bargain!

This was my first venture into satire but since then I have become more cautious because the *Area* article caught the attention of the *Sunday Times* who reviewed it and did a very deadpan-style academic review. In the *Letters to the Editor*, the next week, a reply came from a retired Air Vice Marshall who congratulated me on having the courage to make my suggestion. He said London needed at least six new airports of this size and he modestly pointed out that he had recommended Hyde Park in 1947.

This leads to the point that has emerged. I can imagine no kit of analytical tools that could possibly settle the argument between the Air Vice Marshall and myself. We simply had totally different conceptions of what a desirable London would look like. He clearly felt that a London filled with airports would be wonderful.

What the Roskill Commission (1971) was doing, in effect, was looking at property values and trying to value each bit of the mosaic that comprises the local landscape of, say, Cublington, and then adding them all up to produce a number to represent those potential impacts. But if one went to Christies or Sothebys and attempted to value a Roman mosaic in that fashion, piece by piece, and added all the values to get the mosaic's market value, it would instantly strike everybody as ludicrous. All the individual bits and pieces of a local landscape have links to all the others. There are communities at work that involve interlinkages. There are people with varying degrees of attachment to those communities and this minute examination of the bits and pieces, and then the final aggregation, will be bound to miss the essence of what is at stake.

The 'value' of roads

Getting closer to the present time, the single most important user of benefit-cost analysis in this country in terms of the amount of public money spent based on benefit-cost results is the Department of Transport. All the road building for the last 20 years has been essentially justified using this very simple model.

For any road scheme, analysts calculate user costs on the existing road network over the next 30 years. User costs on the 'improved' network are then estimated and the difference between these – the reduction in user costs from improvement by the scheme – is what they call the user benefit. They then simply subtract the construction costs from the user benefits and discount the difference back to the present and we get the present value of the scheme.

Now, the user costs are essentially three. These are, first, the time saving getting through a traffic jam faster; second, vehicle operating costs savings – the amount of rubber and petrol you consume – and third, traffic-accident reductions. But time savings overwhelmingly dominate everything else, just as they did with Roskill.

So we have the benefits as time saved to motorists to weigh against the road construction costs, and the construction cost includes the acquisition of the land for the new road schemes if land needs buying. Any land acquired is supposed, by the rules of COBA (Department of Transport 1981), to be valued in terms of what it would fetch if offered for sale on the market tomorrow. If you offer a park for sale as a park without planning permission, its market value is pretty low. This, in effect, is how the analysts have been valuing public open space.

This only emerged very recently at an enquiry at Henleys Corner, North London, where we asked the Department of Transport how they would value ten acres of parkland that were going to be taken for that Henleys Corner scheme. The Department was extremely coy about how they did this. We therefore employed a professional valuer to value everything else and we were left in fact with a negative value for the parkland!

A simple illustration of how this method would be applied is a road through a village. Traffic builds up; there is congestion, accidents, stop-and-start driving. The result is a proposal to bypass the village. That bypass relieves congestion in the village, traffic flows freely, saves time and will often save accidents as well, on this particular stretch of road.

But this is another example of horse and rabbit stew, because what is constraining traffic growth in this country – why traffic has hardly grown at all in central London compared to outside London – is the fact that it is being suppressed by total congestion. So relieving congestion bottlenecks fosters a general increase in traffic flow throughout the whole system: more traffic on other roads that are going to have nothing done to them, more danger on roads that are going to have nothing done to them. But these effects lie beyond the boundaries of the model, so they do not count. The Department of Transport only counts the user benefits within a tight little area; the added costs associated with the increase in traffic which is thereby facilitated elsewhere are completely ignored.

Moving to a particular evaluation problem, you find at road enquiries that the analysts have lots of noise-contour maps, showing the amount of noise to be generated by the scheme. It is being proposed – and SACTRA (the Standing Advisory Committee on Trunk Road Assessment) is now looking at the possibility – that COBA should be expanded to embrace environmental variables. One of the hot favourites for inclusion is noise. So it could become the case that you

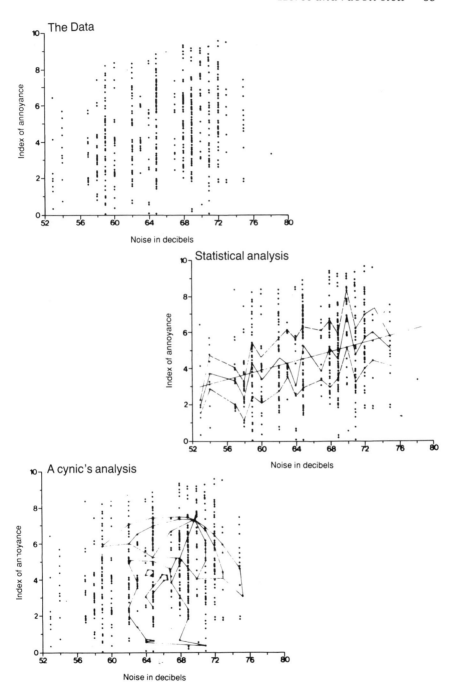

Figure 4.1 The vole in the rain

draw your noise-contour lines, then somehow you attach cash variables to the additional noise generated by the new road and the reduction in noise from where traffic is diverted.

But before we start worrying about how to attach cash values to noise, you have to think about the measurement problems, and what the physical measurements before conversion to cash actually mean. In this respect Figure 4.1 shows a graph that comes from a study which found one of the closest correlations between the physical measures of noise and an index of annoyance. I used to send students up and down the Archway Road, North London, in groups: one group was equipped with questionnaires, with probing questions such as satisfaction with the government, and one question on what they thought of their noise environment. Another group was armed with noise meters to make physical measurements of noise and we always found correlations as impressive as those in Figure 4.1.

Noise meters should properly be referred to as sound-level meters, as noise is unwanted sound and what is one person's music is another person's noise. There is this tendency to equate sound level with noise which misses an extremely important message.

I was involved in another noise-measuring exercise in the early days of Concorde – I was associated with the group that did not like it – and we went to Heathrow airport with noise-measuring equipment. The Department of Trade and Industry were also there with their noise measuring van: they were being very secretive and we were being very open so everybody gathered around us to see what was going on. We measured a few subsonic aircraft first to give some basis of comparison. Then Concorde came over and the reactions on the ground were very interesting. The anti-Concorde group clutched their ears and almost collapsed in agony at the roar of the 'plane. There were other people there, mostly children but some adults, who started leaping and cheering: they thought it was wonderful. Concorde was noisier on the graph but that was not relevant. To one group it was the roar of progress and to the other it was the sound of technology going mad. What the sound-level meters recorded was quite unimportant.

Again we come back to the question that arises time and time again: we have to have a basic framework, a basic consensus of what is acceptable, and so often the forms of analysis I have described are used to try to settle that question rather than try to make decisions within an agreed structure of what is acceptable. Almost invariably nowadays the disagreements about environmental issues can really be traced to fundamental disagreements about the nature of progress itself.

The other hot favourite for inclusion in an extended benefit-cost analysis of road schemes is visual intrusion (by which analysts really mean 'ugliness'). But how do you measure visual intrusion? According to the Department of Transport it is the solid angle subtended at the eye; so you can overlay a grid on whatever structure it is you are proposing to impose on the landscape and from a particular point you can measure the solid angle that will be subtended at the eye and that is the equivalent – the visual intrusion equivalent – of the measurement you get on a sound meter for noise. If you go into the office of any consulting engineer who is making money on road schemes for the Department of Transport you will find the walls of the reception area filled with pictures of their proudest achievements. Yet you could take the pictures off the walls and superimpose visual intrusion grids on them and use them in studies of visual intrusion. The engineers think their roads are splendid architecture; others disagree. Again we have this completely intractable evaluation problem which cannot be settled in a way that would produce numbers useful to settle the larger argument about whether we should have the new roads at all. Likewise the covers on 'girlie' magazines. The economist would say that these are extremely attractive because millions of such magazines are sold each week. Others think them obscene. The solid angle subtended at the eye will not settle that dispute.

Assessment

So where does all this get us? When asked what method would I use instead of benefit-cost analysis, I have said the method used for the 5,000 years before cost-benefit analysis was discovered, namely 'messy politics', which I think is similar to what the Greeks called 'practical wisdom'.

Again in the questions posed in this volume we find the term 'site of environmental value', and the question is whether the ecological matrix is acceptable in determining this value. But the question is, 'acceptable to whom?' Wherever such devices are used you have a conflict which is not a superficial one. The question is not whether the road should go here or there – which is what the Department of Transport always tries to reduce it to with its benefit-cost analysis. None of the major disruption and controversy at motorway enquiries in recent years has been associated with arguments about whether it should be the Red Route or the Green Route as shown on the Department's maps of proposed motorway routes. Classic confrontations like Air Valley, the Winchester Bypass and the Archway Road enquiries have all been between one view of progress, which involves building lots of new motorways, and another view of progress which is exactly the opposite. The arguments were not resolved by analytical methods such as benefit-cost analysis. They were inflamed by them, by their irrelevance.

I have no objection to people producing all the numbers that they find useful in arguing their case, and certainly there are lots of economic numbers that are of genuine value. The ecological matrices and other techniques can also be of genuine value in communicating an argument. But if you are defending something that you think is of *ecological*

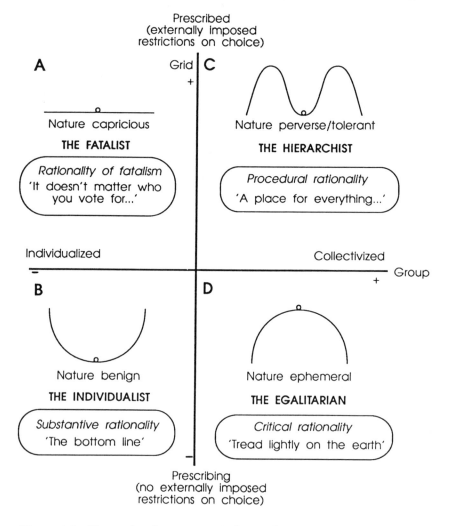

Figure 4.2   The myths of nature mapped on to the rationalities

importance, then again ask yourself how such a label gets attached to something and, more significant, important to whom? Lots of people could not care less about these ecological values. If you are trying to defend something that you value, and if you have attached that label to it, somehow you have to marshal your evidence to garner support from those who really do not care.

To conclude, Figure 4.2 is an attempt to describe some of the actors who are involved in environmental controversies (Schwarz and Thompson 1990). It identifies four myths of nature, with each myth having its adherents. Essentially diagram 'B' is a cup with a ball in it: nature as benign. You can shake it about and the ball always comes back to the bottom of the cup. Diagram 'D', however, is the 'egalitarian's': nature is ephemeral and precarious, such that one shake and all is in ruins. Diagram 'A' represents the 'fatalist's': nature is sometimes good to you, sometimes bad. There is not much that you can do about it except shrug your shoulders and hope for the best. Diagram 'C' is the 'hierarchist's' view: 'nature perverse tolerant' according to Schwarz and Thompson (1990). Within limits you can shake it but if you knock the ball over the rim you are in trouble. These are the large institutions, governments and benefit-cost 'experts' and scientists. All are trying hard to say where those limits are and to devise regulations to keep the ball in the cup. It is useful in any controversy to categorise the actors involved, thereby to try to identify how they will play the analytical games.

References

Adams, J. G. U. (1970) Westminster: The Fourth London Airport? *Area* 2, 1–9.

Department of Transport (1981) *COBA 9 Manual*, London: Department of Transport.

Pearce, D., Markandya, A. and Barbier, E. B. (1989) *Blueprint for a Green Economy*, London: Earthscan Publications.

Roskill, E. W. R. (1971) *Commission on the Third London Airport*, London: HMSO.

Schwarz, M. and Thompson, M. (1990) *Divided we Stand: Redefining Politics, Technology and Social Choice*, London: Harvester Wheatsheaf.

4 Commentary

It is clear that in the 20 years since the Roskill report, a number of factors relating to the evaluation of environmental intangibles have changed. First, an increased level of public awareness of the importance of all the various components of the environment has created a context within which it is necessary to consider collective social values rather than taking market value as the sole measure of value. Second, techniques of BCA have themselves become more sophisticated so that 'extended' analyses have begun to take account of environmental components. As a result, attitudes are beginning to change: the Department of Transport has accepted that market values on their own are not a proxy for the recreational and amenity value of open spaces; in the Aldeburgh study it was accepted that the valuations for ecological sites only represented minimum values. John Adams could not accept, however, that any method had yet been demonstrated as a valid way of measuring intangibles, such as noise, visual intrusion or the importance of wildlife. From his perspective, attaching a monetary value to a grizzly bear is neither realistic nor meaningful. When something is inherently nonsense, increasing the sophistication of methods of measuring it cannot be considered an advance!

An alternative approach is for conservationists to accept that the ends may justify the means, even if they disapprove of those means. From this viewpoint, if a monetary value can be placed on a species, and this results in its preservation, perhaps conservationists should be prepared to tolerate the method to achieve an acceptable outcome. The ends may be considered to justify the means, even if the means are disapproved of.

Nevertheless, Adams' perspective is supported by many ecologists and other environmentalists who believe that there are powerful moral arguments against using BCA and monetary evaluation methods in general for expressing environmental values. Placing a monetary value on something could be taken to imply that its 'owners' can then do what they want with it. A parallel can be drawn between a site of wildlife value and a valuable painting which is individually owned and could be destroyed by its owners if it were not liked. However, this highlights the difference between individual and collective social values. If the painting were owned and therefore 'held in trust' for future generations by the State, there would be no question of destroying it even if it were not appreciated at a particular point in time. Yet this view does not always extend to sites of ecological value. In the case of the proposed Cardiff Bay barrage, for example, the government has recognised the 'value' of the Bay area for its ornithological interest by designating it as a Site of Special Scientific Interest (SSSI). But this concept of its value is presumably not as great as the anticipated benefits from the proposed barrage.

Even if the wildlife value of an area could be expressed in monetary terms, such a figure could not fully reflect all components of the area's value and would leave plenty of opportunity for the benefits of any proposed development to exceed it. There is genuine concern that putting a monetary value on an area could restrict the whole decision-making process to within a CBA framework whereas at present there is scope for public objection to a development on the basis of a wider concept of value which cannot be adequately expressed within a CBA. An additional factor, which often benefits the environment in this process, is that overt public objection may discourage a developer from continuing with a proposed scheme in the face of public protest which could lead to a enquiry and result in costly delays. For these reasons many ecologists fear that once a monetary value is given to a site of ecological interest, it opens the way for arguing that its environmental value had already been adequately represented. The 'messy politics' approach advocated by John Adams may be far from ideal, but at least it leaves the way open for a wider discussion of the concept of environmental value based on collective social values.

One approach to improving the way in which environmental values are taken into account is to have a clearer statement of government policy and priorities, for example in the case of protecting designated areas. This would be of particular benefit at the coast where designations seem to proliferate. Explicit environmental policies can provide valuable support for maintaining sites of environmental importance in the face of development schemes. Similarly, recognition that sites possess values which cannot be expressed in monetary terms may make a more valuable contribution to decision-making processes than attempts to quantify all values in terms of money. It is important to recognise, however, that it is unlikely that full consensus on the total value of a particular site can ever be reached and there will always be potential for some conflict over valuation in a pluralist society where many groups hold different things to be of value.

It is becoming increasingly clear that environmental matters are now important to a wider section of society than formerly and that this makes the issue of how to express concepts of environmental value even more urgent. There is less agreement over whether this should be done by placing monetary values on ecological and other components of the environment, or by developing ways of expressing collective social values in non-monetary terms in the decision-making process. There is more general agreement that it would be better to explore several different approaches. What is clear is that, in view of the high profile of environmental concerns at present, it could well be important to develop both quantitative and non-quantitative approaches to expressing environmental values.

5 Valuing the benefits of coastal defence: a case study of the Aldeburgh sea-defence scheme

R. K. Turner, I. Bateman and J. S. Brooke

Introduction

Benefit estimation involves the placing of money values on the gains and losses from economic activity. Benefit estimation has long been part of the public project appraisal process in the UK, but only relatively recently has it been extended to include environmental impacts. The Ministry of Agriculture, Fisheries and Food (MAFF) grant-aids schemes designed to protect coastal assets from inundation, flooding and erosion by the sea. Before grant aid is approved such sea defence schemes are required to demonstrate that their social benefits (in terms of damage costs avoided) are greater than their social costs (capital construction and running costs).

In 1988 a study was undertaken by the Environmental Appraisal Group at the University of East Anglia in order to carry out an economic benefits assessment of a proposed sea defence scheme for Aldeburgh on the Suffolk coast. This chapter reviews the methodology that was devised for the Aldeburgh study, including environmental and recreational impacts. Given the limited timescale available for the study, a fairly pragmatic approach to valuation was adopted. Every effort was, however, made to produce 'conservative' benefit estimates.

Description of benefits area at risk

Aldeburgh lies at the south-eastern heel of East Anglia. Figure 5.1 shows the benefits area evaluated in this analysis. In 1988 the sea defences south of Aldeburgh consisted of a piled concrete wall fronted by a dilapidated groyne system extending southwards from Fort Green

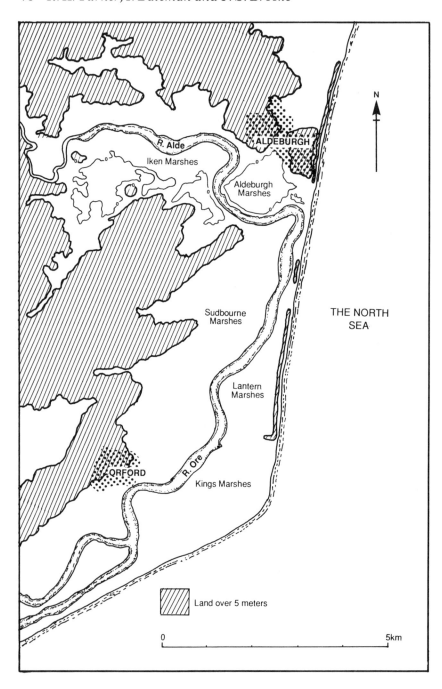

Figure 5.1   Study area

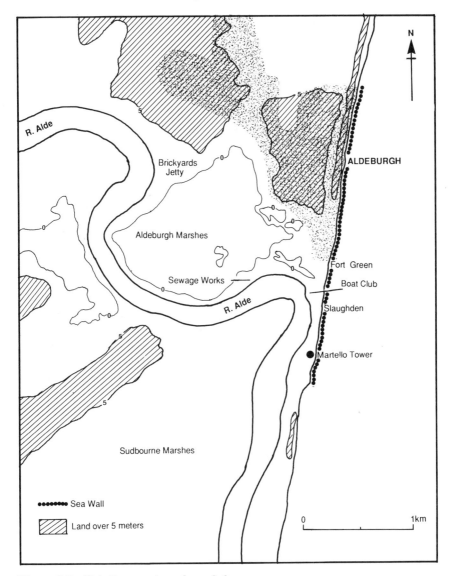

Figure 5.2 Existing assets and sea defences

for approximately 1,400 metres (see Figure 5.2). The natural shingle structure of Orfordness starts at the termination of this wall as a narrow shingle bank that broadens to form the Lantern and then the King's Marshes which are owned by the Ministry of Defence.

Recession of the natural beach had removed material from in front of the concrete wall and had formed a step in the alignment of the

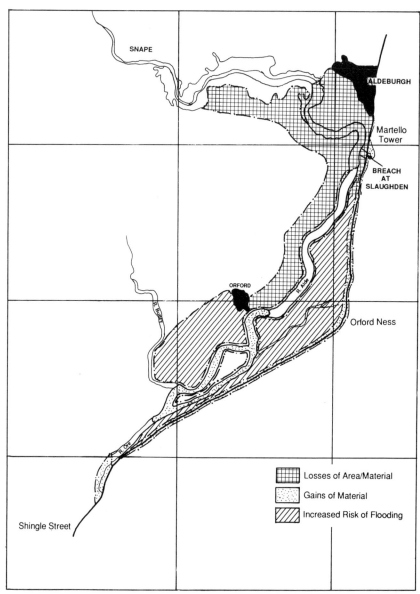

source: (Dobbie 1986) (b)

Figure 5.3   The consequences of a breach at Slaughden

foreshore at the end of the wall, the wall having acted locally to restrict the landward movement of the high water line.

Construction of the existing defences was begun shortly after the 1953 floods and completed in 1955. To limit expenditure the wall was constructed with a high toe level. Along the southern section of the wall in particular, the low beach levels had exposed the steel piled toe to frequent and aggressive attack by the sea. Shingle entrained by the sea is impacted on the piling, causing a rapid reduction in thickness. The toe piling had a number of large holes through it which had allowed material to be washed from beneath the wall. Large voids existed which in some cases extended from the toe piles to the rear support piles. Regular emergency maintenance works costing £70,000–£100,000 per annum were necessary to prevent the failure of the wall and the development of a breach.

A partial collapse did occur in February 1988 when voiding under three bays to the south of the Martello Tower became so extensive that all support under the apron was lost and the wall rotated forwards and downwards causing the failure of the rear piled supports. An expensive emergency grouting operation was necessary to stabilise the wall and preserve the integrity of the defences in the short term.

The narrow unprotected shingle spit to the south of the concrete wall was another area where the development of a breach was considered likely under rough sea conditions. Recession of the foreshore on this narrow neck frequently causes a reduction in the height of the natural shingle bank and the emergency works here have included the importation of large quantities of shingle to reform the bank to an adequate height.

The defence policy of emergency maintenance works only succeeded in providing the most fragile of defence lines. In addition, these works would have become more expensive as further recession of the coastline continued, and in the long term would be unable to protect against a breach without major capital expenditure.

Figure 5.3 illustrates the likely consequences of a breach at Slaughden. Following the failure of the existing sea defences, a breach up to 200 metres wide was likely to develop. At this width the estuary would have been open to wave action which would impinge directly on the eastern river walls protecting the Sudbourne marshes. These walls would quickly be overwhelmed, the land permanently inundated and low-lying areas within Orford village would have been exposed to frequent flooding.

The increased turbulence in the estuary and reflected wave action would also cause rapid erosion and eventual failure of the Aldeburgh marsh wall, putting at risk up to 97 properties at the southern end of

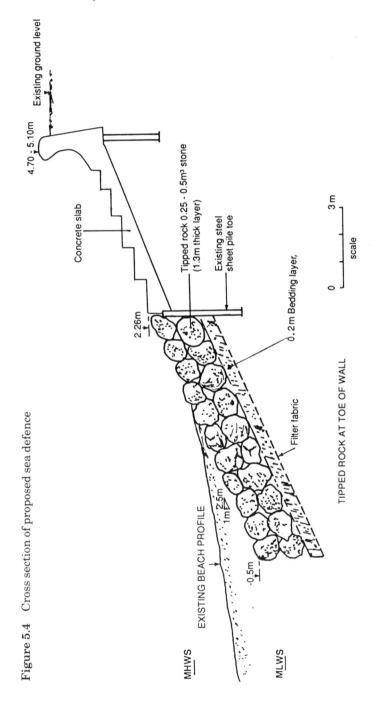

Figure 5.4   Cross section of proposed sea defence

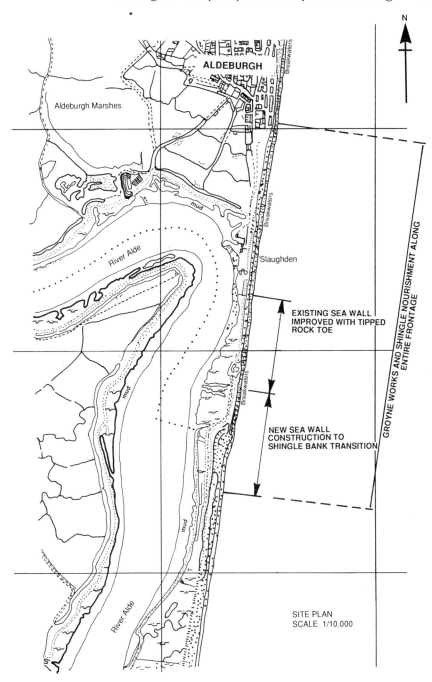

Figure 5.5   Proposed sea defence developments

Aldeburgh. The wall was last breached in such circumstances during the major tidal surge which occurred on 31 January/1 February 1953 when the marshes were inundated to depths of over 3.5 metres and properties flooded up to depths of 1.5 metres.

Proposed scheme

It was suggested that to improve the performance of the existing sea wall a tipped rock toe apron (see Figure 5.4) would be constructed as an extension of the present sea wall toe along the southern part of the frontage up to a point 300 metres north of the Martello Tower. It was also proposed that the most badly deteriorated section of existing wall at the southern end would be demolished and replaced by a new sea wall extending a further 150m south of the existing wall. In addition a programme of groyne renewal and shingle nourishment was proposed to extend from Fort Green south to the end of the new wall (see Figure 5.5).

Benefits estimation methodology

The methodology employed was conventional cost-benefit analysis (CBA) based on economic efficiency criteria. The proposed sea defence scheme will have primary economic efficiency implications, environmental and social/distributional implications. These will be both positive and negative.

Economic analysis using CBA techniques must be distinguished from financial analysis. Economic analysis is concerned with the gains or losses to the nation as a whole from a particular scheme, and not solely those to the individuals or organisations undertaking and/or affected by the scheme. *Economic* gains or losses are not therefore the sum of individual financial gains or losses, because one individual may gain as a direct result of another losing. For example, if a shop loses business because of flooding, then that shop's customers may simply shop elsewhere; the first shop's loss is another's gain.

In standard CBA undertaken for grant-aid purposes, the norm is to count only national economic efficiency impacts. Thus financial losses suffered locally, and which could be wholly offset by counter-balancing gains elsewhere within the nation, cannot be counted as national economic losses.

Two basic engineering options have been appraised in the cost benefit analysis:

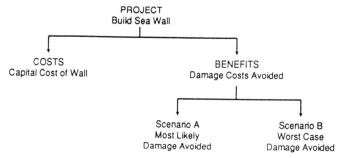

Scenario A - Most Likely

i)   Year 1:   Incomplete failure of sea wall at Slaughden.
ii) Year 2-5: Developing breach at Slaughden, major changes affecting assets behind the sea wall within the vicinity of the breach. Orfordness and Havergate Island will face increased risk of flooding. Deposition/siltation after year 40.
iii) Year 6:   Complete breach at Slaughden, failure of Sudbourne Marsh Wall, 1 in 6 year flooding of Gedgrave Marsh.
iv) Year 10:   Failure of river wall protecting Aldeburgh Town Marsh.
v)   Year 20:   Gedgrave Marsh wall fails.

Notes:
   a)   Breach at Slaughden not expected to exacerbate already weak position at Iken Marshes.
   b)   No implications for other marshes around rivers Alde, Ore and Butley.

Scenario B - Worst Case

i)   Year 1·   Complete breach at Slaughden. Failure of walls at Sudbourne and Aldeburgh Town Marshes. Increased flood risk to Gedgrave Marsh. Havergate Island and Orfordness face increased risk of flooding.
ii) Year 5:   Gedgrave Marsh wall fails.
iii) Year 20:   Increased siltation around Havergate Island and Orfordness.

Figure 5.6   Cost benefit analysis – Aldeburgh sea defence scheme

1) a 'do nothing' option;
2) a full capital work scheme.

The 'do nothing' option would result in increasing costs over time due to both flood damage and changes in the current patterns of erosion and accretion. Two scenarios have been considered in order to evaluate the consequences of allowing the sea wall to fail. Scenario A is based on a timescale judged at the time (1987/88) to be 'most likely' by the consulting engineers. It assumes a gradual failure of the sea and river defences. Scenario B is based on a 'worst case' sequence of events in which both the sea wall and some river walls fail completely and at approximately the same time. These two scenarios obviously result in different benefit (damage costs avoided) profiles over time (see Figure 5.6).

For many goods and services (private goods) there are no difficulties in establishing market values (via market prices, adjusted or unadjusted) of their worth. But a significant proportion of environmental goods and services, such as clean air and water, landscape and amenity, etc. tend, however, to fall into the category of public or quasi-public goods (see Figure 5.7). At present monetary values cannot be derived for all the environmental effects a given scheme may induce. In order to derive monetary value estimates for quasi-private, quasi-public or public goods, it is necessary to use some form of procedure which can simulate or substitute for the missing market prices.

Four different methodological approaches, two direct (a and b) and two indirect (c and d), have been suggested in the literature for securing money measures of environmental benefits/damages in the absence of markets (Pearce and Turner 1990):

a) identification of surrogate markets, e.g. the degree to which amenity and environmental quality attributes are reflected in property and land prices (hedonic pricing), or travel costs incurred by recreational amenity users;
b) market 'creation' via questionnaire-based methods such as the contingent valuation method;
c) dose-response data linked to valuation; productivity losses, replacement and substitute costs; and
d) public preference value identification using expert opinion and/or political weights.

In the context of the Aldeburgh sea defence scheme there were few benefits in the form of increased provision of goods or services. Instead benefits are mainly in the form of losses avoided. Specifically we are concerned with the benefit of avoiding flood damage to a range of items. These include:

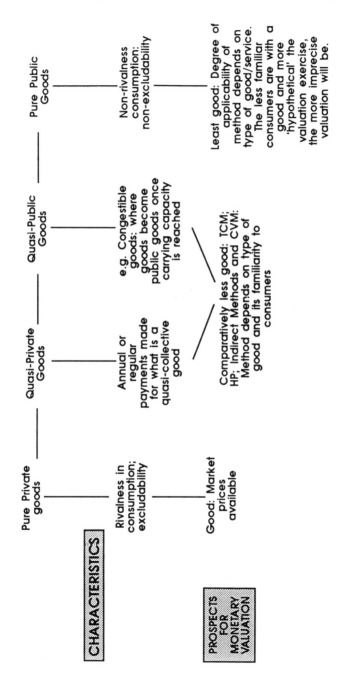

Figure 5.7   Valuation of goods and services

i)   Agricultural output losses avoided;
ii) Expected property damage costs avoided;
iii) Environmental damage avoided;
iv) Recreational/Heritage losses avoided.

Most of these items are evaluated by reference to existing market prices, e.g. the value of lost agricultural output, the damage cost of flooded properties. Such techniques are referred to as 'indirect' methods as they do not directly obtain the local population's valuation of 'willingness to pay' for damage avoidance.

Such techniques are clearly inappropriate where market prices do not exist. So, for example, in the valuation of recreational losses we employ 'direct' valuation techniques such as the contingent valuation (or survey) method to obtain a direct measure of an individuals 'willingness to pay'. We can illustrate the various techniques by looking at each benefit category in turn.

Benefit valuation 1 – agricultural loss avoided (indirect method)

Three marsh areas, Sudbourne, Gedgrave and Aldeburgh, were considered vulnerable to flooding and saline inundation. Due to a lack of natural barriers, once a marsh wall fails the entire marsh is flooded. (Iken marsh is subject to flooding irrespective of a sea wall breach.)

Two levels of flood damage were considered:

Infrequent flooding – minor breach (years 0–5 Scenario A)
Inundation – from a major/permanent breach (years 6+ Scenario A; years 1+ Scenario B)

Furthermore two farming regimes were identified: irrigated and non-irrigated cropping. This difference was important because it led to differing crop yields/values. Therefore we obtained a simple damage matrix.

| | Farm Water Regime | |
	Not Irrigated	Irrigated
Infrequent flooding	£W/ha	£X/ha
Inundation	£Y/ha	£Z/ha

Finally there was also the possibility of increased saline intrusion into the water supplies utilised by irrigated agriculture outside the flood plain. Here two approaches to loss evaluation were taken. Where alternative (say deeper) sources of non-saline irrigation water are available then the costs of such alternative supplies provide a measure of the benefits afforded by preventing saline intrusion occurring. Where such an alternative water source is not available then the

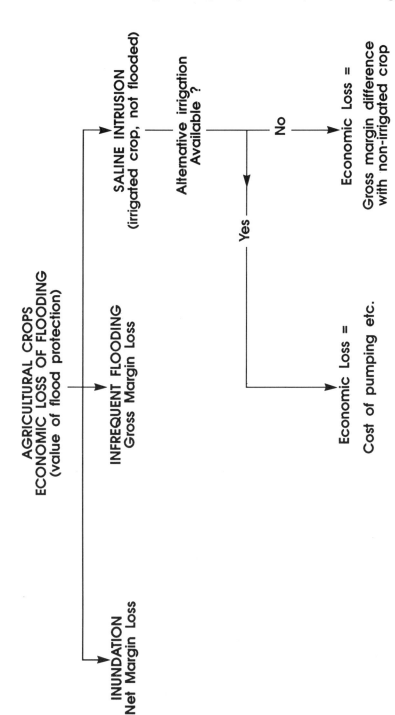

Figure 5.8 Benefit valuation 1 – agricultural loss avoided

farming regime must switch to non-irrigated crops, resulting (presumably) in a lower value crop. Here the difference between the pre- and post-breach gross margin gives us a measure of the value of flood protection. Figure 5.8 summarises the agricultural evaluation approaches adopted.

Benefit valuation 2 – property damage avoided (indirect method)

Work by Dobbie (1986a and b), Penning-Rowsell (1978), Parker et al. (1983) and Turner and Brooke (1988) was supplemented with data from the Anglian Water Authority to calculate post-breach flood depths and return periods. Damage valuation was then made by reference to Middlesex Polytechnic's (Flood Hazard Research Centre) publication 'Potential Flood Damage Data: A Major Update' (Suleman et al. 1988). This relates flood return period to likely damage intensity.

eg.   Return Period : 1 in 10 years
gives   Average Flood Depth : 0.6m depth
and   Average Flood Duration : >12 hours

These damage estimates are applied to data covering the age and type of property affected in order to obtain a monetary depth/damage valuation.

Benefit valuation 3 – environmental damage avoided (indirect method)

Figure 5.9 illustrates environmental interest in the area. The entire area is designated as an Area of Outstanding Natural Beauty. However, three categories of environmental interest were considered particularly relevant to the area:

a) Environmentally Sensitive Area – all the land subject to post-breach flooding has ESA certification and local farmers are in receipt of payments under this scheme in return for environmentally sensitive land management;

b) Site of Special Scientific Interest – Orfordness, Havergate Island and the River Butley valley have SSSI status, being the largest and best preserved area of vegetated shingle in Britain;

c) National Nature Reserve – Havergate Island and the southern peninsula of Orfordness enjoy both NNR and Special Protection Area (SPA) designation and meet the criteria for Ramsar designation (i.e. wetlands of international significance under the convention on Wetlands of International Importance, Ramsar, 1971).

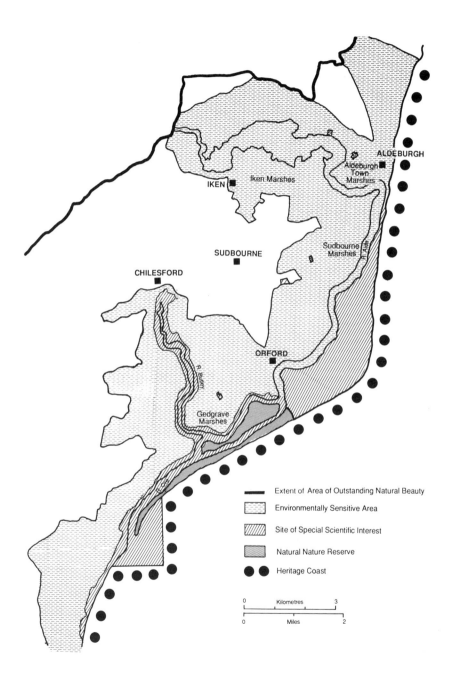

Figure 5.9   Environmental interest

Valuation of ESA

The ecological and landscape value of the ESA area has already been proxied via the ESA payment scheme. This gives an example of a public preference value as reflected through the political process. This is an overt acceptance of the political process as the arbiter of public valuation and is as representative as is that process.

Valuation of SSSI

English Nature (formerly the NCC), currently own the southern part of Orfordness (100 ha under joint SSSI/NNR designation) but had expressed an interest in purchasing a further 316 ha at the current market price, and in ultimately purchasing the entire land area of Orfordness so that the whole SSSI could be safeguarded against adverse change.

Using the per ha valuation, a market value for the whole of Orfordness can be derived. In the absence of any precise information about the actual rate of deterioration that would be suffered by the environmental asset (Orfordness) following a breach, it was assumed that the area would be of negligible value by the end of the study time horizon (50 years). Given this assumption, an annual depreciation loss was evaluated. No loss was included for agriculture on Orfordness as after investigation this proved to be operating with negative net margins (sustained by grants alone). Therefore its loss would not be an economic loss to the nation.

Valuation of NNR

The part of the NNR located on the southern spit of Orfordness is dealt with above. This leaves Havergate Island (108 ha). This was purchased by the RSPB in 1948 to provide a safe nesting site for the Avocet among other birds.

The island contains several artificial lagoons regulated by sluices which are managed to maintain depth and regulate salinity. The increase in peak water levels following a sea-wall breach would increase flood risk and result in higher defensive and management costs. Currently the RSPB contract-in machinery. However, with higher flood return periods, the purchase of machinery becomes a cheaper option. A sea-wall breach would therefore force the RSPB into both the occasional purchase of walling and pumping machinery and into spending more on maintenance costs. These additional costs (defensive expenditures) were entered as the relevant economic loss associated with post-breach damage to Havergate Island.

Benefit valuation 4 – heritage/recreational losses avoided (indirect/direct methods)

Figure 5.10 shows that the items at risk from flood damage can be divided into site specific and non site specific categories.

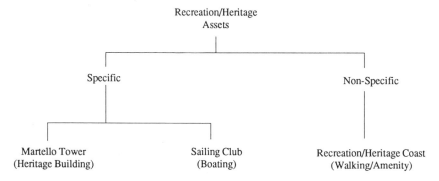

Figure 5.10   Recreation and heritage assets

In each case we need to ascertain whether potential losses are true national economic losses or whether they would simply result in individuals moving to use other local regional alternatives, i.e. are substitutes available, and if so are the alternative boat clubs or recreation assets adequate substitutes? If the answer is yes then there are no economic costs (apart from the extra resource costs involved in switching consumption to the alternative) to enter in the CBA. If the answer is no then economic costs do arise and they require evaluation.

Martello Tower (indirect method)

The Martello Tower at Aldeburgh represents the northern extremity of the Napoleonic coastal defences built between 1810 and 1812. In 1971 it was purchased, in very poor condition, by the Landmark Trust and restored to its original condition. As such it is possibly the finest of the 13 surviving towers. Valuation of the loss of the Tower was estimated by calculating the cost of purchasing and fully restoring one of the other 12 towers in the national stock. This is admittedly a slight underestimate as such an option would leave the stock of towers diminished by one.

Yachting and sailing clubs (indirect method)

A yacht club, a sailing club and a number of boat yards are situated to the rear of the sea wall on the river Alde. A sea wall failure at Slaughden would have necessitated the abandonment of all these sites.

The clubs themselves provide the only base facilities serving the very high demand for sailing on the rivers Alde and Ore. However, providing that alternative facilities can be offered at other clubs within a reasonable distance, then the local flood loss of facilities would only have represented a transfer of use rather than a national loss, i.e. no economic cost would be entered in the CBA.

In this case, however, it was found that marinas/clubs were fully booked with long waiting lists. It was therefore not feasible for the majority of sailors to move to an alternative club and enjoy an equivalent recreational experience. There were grounds, therefore, for arguing that no adequate substitute facilities were available in the region and to this extent the estimated costs of relocating the clubs represented true 'economic' costs which could legitimately be included in the CBA calculations.

A completely suitable alternative site is not available in the locality. However, a site at the Aldeburgh Brickworks upstream of the river Alde (see Figure 5.2) could provide the necessary mooring provided that a new marina was constructed.

Two evaluations were prepared. The first only included the cost of relocating facilities from Slaughden to the Brickworks without building the marina. Although, because of the lack of mooring at the brickworks site, such an option is physically inadequate it does provide some hypothetical value associated with the existing 'ability to sail'. The second evaluation included the alternative construction of a marina at the Brickyards to provide sufficient additional mooring space to fully accommodate the transfer of all the craft presently moored at Slaughden.

Recreational and heritage coast assets (direct method)

Unlike the benefit estimate items (e.g. agricultural crops, relocation of boat club, etc.) there is no market price to which we can refer for an indirect evaluation of recreation. Instead we must refer directly to the actions and evaluations of the individuals concerned.

There are several direct techniques for the evaluation of unpriced environmental goods. However, the most widely applied, and that chosen at Aldeburgh, is the Contingent Valuation Method (CVM). This is an expressed preference survey method which involves asking individuals, in a structured way, what they are willing to pay (WTP) for an environmental gain and/or what they are willing to accept (WTA) by way of compensation to tolerate an environmental loss. As such this is a 'direct' evaluation method and, as its name implies, involves the construction of a contingent (or hypothetical) market for the environmental good (here recreation).

There are a number of problems and advantages to CVM. Common criticisms include:

1. Validation – Since hypotheses can never be proved, only negated, the resultant evaluations can only be 'weakly' validated by other direct techniques (convergent validity), or by the incorporation of, for example, attitude theory tests in the survey vehicle;
2. Novelty – Individuals are unused to valuing unpriced environmental goods, assessing contingent markets and determining WTP;
3. WTP/WTA – Asymmetry, although this may not be a problem but a psychological norm;
4. Reliability
   problems – Various types of bias:
   a) Strategic: free rider, incentive to over/understate;
   b) Hypothetical: unfamiliarity with asset or valuation of the asset;
   c) Vehicle: payment mode;
   d) Starting point: the influence of how the bidding procedure is actually undertaken.

However, CVM also has many advantages. Many of the problems are survey problems not specific to CVM and are now being addressed. Furthermore CVM often provides the only ball-park estimate of unpriced goods which are unamendable to alternative valuation techniques.

Survey research requires careful attention to the problem of conveying meaning to diverse respondents and monitoring them to ensure that they undertake the effort necessary to arrive at an evaluation. A successful CVM scenario must be understandable by the respondent in the terms intended by the researcher and be perceived as plausible and meaningful.

The Aldeburgh CVM set out to minimise bias problems. The questionnaire provided information concerning local sea defences, environmental assets and individuals' current taxation/rates contributions. The aim was to minimise hypothetical bias. Furthermore individuals were asked WTP via taxes without iterative bidding in an attempt to prevent vehicle or starting point bias. It was recognised that strategic bias may have been a problem. However, the payment scenarios presented were realistic and the majority of empirical studies undertaken in the 1980s suggested that strategic bias was the most minor bias problem (Pearce et al. 1989).

The survey related to visitors to Aldeburgh Sea Wall and at Orford Quay. Three categories of individuals were identified:

1) Locals;
2) Non-locals – who felt the resource gave unique benefits to them;
3) Non-locals – who felt that viable alternative sites existed for them.

The number of group visits per category was calculated and the CVM was used to estimate WTP per group for the recreational benefits enjoyed.

For Category 3 (Non-local/not unique asset) the loss of the wall and environs would not represent an economic loss as they could visit an alternative site without loss of enjoyment. However, they would have to travel further to alternative sites. In this case a simple Travel Distance Cost evaluation was carried out. An estimate of extra distance was obtained. The extra fuel cost was calculated and this was entered as the economic cost of the resource loss for this group. An alternative evaluation was also estimated using the Department of Transport's value of time (assuming an average travel speed of 50 km.p.h.).

It was recognised that the loss of recreational benefits would be a gradual process related to the rate of amenity quality loss at the site. Sensitivity analysis was carried out to model a number of different rates of asset decline.

Conclusion

CBA results
Under both Scenario A and B the CBA produced benefits in excess of costs. The results were accepted by the regional water authority and

scheme development plans were subsequently funded by MAFF. At the time of writing, phase 1 of the development is nearing completion.

Appendix 1

The nature of value
The CVM survey was undertaken with visitors to Aldeburgh Sea Wall and at Orford Quay. This means that only those individuals who actually use the resource have a say in its valuation. This is not necessarily the complete set of people who value the assets, as those who do not visit the site may still value the site's existence. Some individuals may wish to see the site preserved so that they and/or others retain an option to visit it. Others may not wish to visit Aldeburgh themselves but would want to see the assets retained for future generations (bequest value). Finally some may feel that environmental assets such as the abundant birdlife of the area or local beach flowers have a value which derives purely from their existence.

We can see then that for both visitors and non-visitors the total value of the site at Aldeburgh is a composite of several different classes of value. We term this 'Total Economic Value' (TEV) and subdivide its components as follows:

i) Primary Use Value: the use value which is the prime objective of an asset, e.g. the flood protection properties of the sea wall.

ii) Secondary Use Value: the downstream (or upstream) user values generated by assets, e.g. the sea wall is designed to prevent flooding but might also protect navigation along the river thus promoting trade (not shown to be a factor at Aldeburgh). Recreation can be classed as a secondary value deriving from the sea wall.

iii) Option Use Value: the value which individuals place on having the option to use a resource, e.g. willingness to pay to preserve the option of recreation at Aldeburgh.

iv) Bequest Value: the value which individuals derive from ensuring that a resource is preserved for use by successive generations, e.g. preserving the Havergate Island bird sanctuary for one's children to enjoy. This is a non-use value with respect to the present generation individual (but a use value for future generations).

v) Existence Value: individuals may express a value for things which have no use value for either themselves or succeeding generations. This is a value expressed purely for the continued existence of the item, therefore this is again a non-use value, e.g. individuals may express a willingness to pay to preserve a species of deep ocean plant life simply because they believe in the preservation of all flora and fauna.

Figure 5.11 summarises the above value parts.

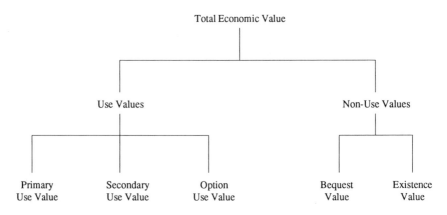

Figure 5.11   Components of total economic value

Appendix 2

Alternative value relationships
The Aldeburgh case study draws upon human valuations to evaluate a variety of economic and environmental assets. Two factors can be ascribed to the formation of human values: first, people act as individuals; second they act as members of society, i.e. humans have individual and social (or public) preferences. For example, a person's individual preference may be an expansion of the highway system while their public preference is for preservation of the environment.

The private preference system is most clearly articulated through market forces and the determination of market prices. In the Aldeburgh case study, private preferences (market prices) are the basis for the evaluation of agricultural losses because it is market prices which determine gross margins. However where there are market failures (resulting from non-competitive market structures, information gaps or externalities) or where no market exists (unpriced goods) then market prices become an unreliable or unobtainable means of estimating private preferences. In such cases Cost Benefit Analysis attempts to estimate individual valuations through the preferences explicitly expressed by individuals in surveys (e.g. CVM) or implicitly revealed preferences by individuals' consumption or related goods (e.g. Travel Costs Methods).

A quite different standpoint is being adopted in the evaluation of the environmental/amenity value of the designated ESA. In accepting the Government's ESA payment level as the environmental value of the ESA, we are utilising an expressed public preference value. This is being determined by Government who are the elected arbiters of public preference values.

Pearce and Turner (1990) suggest that in addition to the basic division between private and public preference systems, environmental values may also be viewed in non-preference terms, i.e. purely

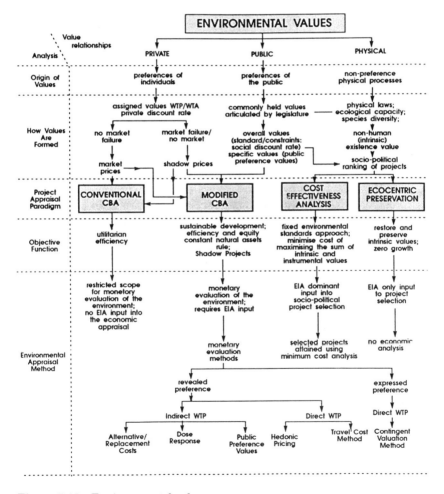

Figure 5.12 Environmental values

in terms of the physical processes and systems which they embody. Such a concept extends the human orientated value basis of TEV to allow for the possibility of non-human values, e.g. the right of a species to exist in its own right, devoid of any human non-use existence value. To date, however, there are no practical methods for the evaluation of such a non-human existence value and no attempt to do so is undertaken in this study.

Figure 5.12 summarises the differing philosophical standpoints and value relationships which constitute these evaluation systems.

References

Dobbie and Partners (1986a) *Aldeburgh Sea Defences: Part 1 Report*, Volumes I-III, Croydon: Dobbie and Partners.

Dobbie and Partners (1986b) *Aldeburgh Sea Defences: The 'Do-Nothing' Alternative*, Croydon: Dobbie and Partners.

Parker, D. J., Green, C. H. and Penning-Rowsell, E. C. (1983) *Swalecliffe Coast Protection Proposals: Evaluation of Potential Benefits*, Enfield: Flood Hazard Research Centre.

Pearce, D. W., Markandya, A. and Barbier, E. B. (1989) *Blueprint for a Green Economy*, London: Earthscan.

Pearce, D. W. and Turner, R. K. (1990) *Economics of Natural Resources and the Environment*, Hemel Hempstead: Harvester Wheatsheaf.

Penning-Rowsell, E. C. (1978) *The Effect of Salt Contamination on Flood Damage to Residential Properties*, Enfield: Flood Hazard Research Centre.

Suleman, M. S., N'Jai, A., Green, C. H. and Penning-Rowsell, E. C. (1988) *Potential Flood Damage Data: A Major Update*, Enfield: Flood Hazard Research Centre.

Turner, R. K. and Brooke, J. (1988) *Cost-Benefit Analysis of the Lower Bure, Halvergate Fleet and Acle Marshes I.D.B. Flood Protection Scheme*, Norwich: Environmental Appraisal Group, University of East Anglia.

Turner, R. K. and Pearce, D. W. (1990) *The Ethical Foundations of Sustainable Economic Development*, London: International Institute for Environment and Development, University College London.

5 Commentary

This case study provides an interesting example of the integrated application of methods for valuing different components of the environment. However, there was considerable debate over whether the basic assumptions, which had been made before the benefit-cost analysis (BCA) had been carried out, were correct. It was argued that the BCA had been carried out with the assumption that the particular environment which was present at Aldeburgh at this specific moment in time *should* be protected, and that the figures had been used only to support that argument. Would it have been possible for another BCA to have been carried out, using different assumptions, to have come to a different conclusion? It was suggested that the BCA gave the impression of justifying a certain pre-determined level of scheme expenditure rather than objectively appraising the costs and benefits of the proposed scheme. This leads to questioning whether more benefits would have been added if there had been insufficient to justify the pre-determined scheme with the components considered. The research team made it clear that BCA must be regarded as a tool to aid decision-making. The result of an analysis is not an absolute measure of economic efficiency and does not constitute a decision in itself. Other factors outside the analysis can be incorporated into the process of decision-making. For example an unfavourable BC ratio can still result in a scheme going ahead if that political decision has already been taken. Conversely a favourable BC ratio would not necessarily mean that scheme would definitely go ahead.

Ian Bateman stressed that the values arrived at for environmental goods were minimum values. It was pointed out that it should not be implied that the ecological value of the area had been assessed.

A major limitation of taking land values as a measure of economic value is that as far as the purchase of land is concerned English Nature (formerly the NCC), has to work to Treasury guidelines so that the purchase price of land for wildlife conservation purposes is based on the District Valuer's valuation. The purchase price cannot be taken as equivalent to the ecological value of a site as the valuation is not a reflection of ecological value. Indeed, it is questionable whether land values should even be used as a surrogate for ecological values since they are more likely to reflect the agricultural value of the land which is, in many cases, the converse of its ecological value. For example, a wet meadow with poor productivity will have a low agricultural value but a high ecological value due to the diversity of plant and animal species it supports.

The method of using Environmentally Sensitive Area (ESA) payments as a surrogate for ecological value is similarly open to objection because of the links with agricultural values. The ESA payments which a farmer receives to maintain traditional agricultural practices cover a five year period and doubts also exist over the validity of this as a measure of value.

A further limitation of the approach was that no evaluation was included for the cultural associations of the area – the art, literature and music, in particular the music of Britten. As much of the area is covered by different statutory designations, such as AONB, this could be taken to represent an implicit value placed on it by the government, yet this was not explicitly recognised in the study.

Another criticism of the study is that it operated within a narrow framework which failed to consider the 'do nothing' option. If a BCA had been undertaken for this option it would have brought a completely different perspective to bear. Instead of designing a scheme to protect the existing ecological value of the area, another policy option could have been to allow a breach to occur on the basis that new habitats would thereby be created. One reason for considering such a measure is that much of the area has been modified by human activities, especially to the north of the National Nature Reserve, and although it undoubtedly contains a number of different elements of environmental value, it has been suggested that allowing new habitats to form could result in sites of at least an equivalent if not a greater value. Although the Royal Society for the Protection of Birds' (RSPB) reserve at Orfordness would be lost in the event of a breach, one prediction is that an avocet nesting area three times the present one could be created. It was agreed that the majority of ecologists might well advocate protection of the 'status quo' because they have been thrown into a defensive mode of considering site protection as the only means of wildlife conservation. This is the result of a history of trying to prevent development, rather than taking into account the dynamics of natural systems and their potential for site evolution and change. As far as coastlines are concerned, the dynamic nature of natural processes should be increasingly recognised. An overall policy of arresting long-term coastal change would be far too expensive in the long run in any case.

Similarly, for recreation benefits the study did not appear to have considered the 'do nothing' options sufficiently. The major benefits – as calculated – were associated with the yacht club, yet if a breach were to occur a harbour easily accessible to the sea would be created. This would create a new scenario with a different type of boat use with comparable if not greater benefits for recreational boating overall, although it should be noted that a different group of boat users would be the main beneficiaries, i.e. cruisers rather than dinghies.

Finally, Aldeburgh is an important location in geomorphological terms, in European and global terms as well as nationally, yet this component of environmental value was not considered by the study. A scheme including an extension of the sea wall would cause further erosion by preventing longshore drift in the future. This could be particularly problematic because Orfordness is very narrow at this point since the construction of groynes further up the coast has previously prevented sediment from being carried to the site. Such a strategy would undermine the geomorphological value of the area. This illustrates a major problem in coastal management from an environmental point of view. It tends to be dominated by engineers who, as a result of their training, generally prefer 'hard' engineering solutions although there are increasingly 'soft' environmentally sensitive alternatives.

In summary, many ecologists could see considerable drawbacks involved in the use of BCA as a decision-making tool given these limitations. In this particular study, they felt that not only were most features of 'intrinsic' environmental value not included but the underlying assumptions with regard to the definition of the area and of the problem could be questioned. It is always difficult to reach a decision which is in the best interests of all concerned. However, omitting problematic aspects from the benefit cost analysis will not diffuse the need to incorporate some allowance for their value into the decision-making process.

6 Survey-based valuation methods

S. M. Tunstall and A. Coker

Approaches to the economic valuation of environmental value

The value that an environment possesses has many different components, not all of which will be held equally important by different groups in society. In order to consider how these various components might be valued, they have been divided into three categories: utilitarian, user and intrinsic, according to the type of function they perform (Figure 6.1). In practice, it is not so straightforward to allocate all components of environmental value to categories according to their function, as categories may overlap or be inadequate. For example, a different approach might make a distinction between 'existence for its own sake' independent of human values, and the other components of the 'intrinsic' category (Tunstall, Green and Lord 1988).

For functions in the first category, the utilitarian component, we can generally use direct or indirect market mechanisms to put a monetary value on them. In the case of the second category, the user component, we now have considerable experience in the application of Contingent Valuation Methods to give values in money terms to components of use that had previously been considered as 'environmental intangibles'. However, we are only just beginning to look at how to approach the valuation of functions in the third category, the intrinsic components.

The most easily measured of the utilitarian functions are those associated with commercial production, the value of which can be measured directly in money terms, for example, the market value of fish harvested. Others may be at least partially valued in indirect terms, such as the cost of seeking alternative fishing grounds when spawning grounds have been destroyed. However, due to the complexities of biological systems it is unlikely that it will ever be possible to measure direct causal relationships in such cases. There will always be an element of 'knock-on effect', sometimes of considerable economic importance, where actions in one area destroy

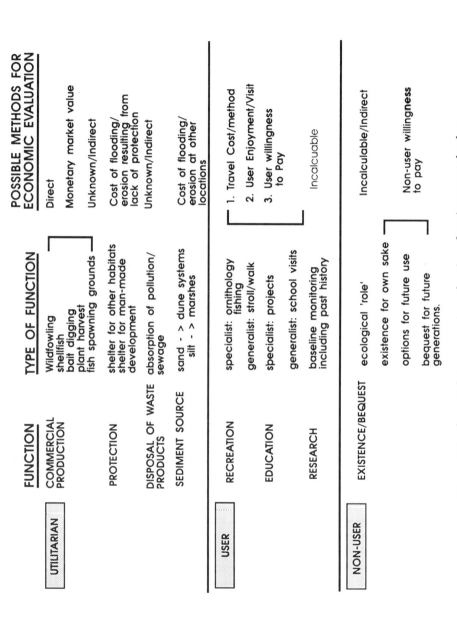

Figure 6.1 Approach to economic evaluation of environmental value

FUNCTION	TYPE OF FUNCTION	POSSIBLE METHODS FOR ECONOMIC EVALUATION
UTILITARIAN		
COMMERCIAL PRODUCTION	Wildfowling shellfish bait digging plant harvest fish spawning grounds	Direct Monetary market value Unknown/Indirect
PROTECTION	shelter for other habitats shelter for man-made development	Cost of flooding/ erosion resulting from lack of protection
DISPOSAL OF WASTE PRODUCTS	absorption of pollution/ sewage	Unknown/Indirect
SEDIMENT SOURCE	sand − > dune systems silt − > marshes	Cost of flooding/ erosion at other locations
USER		
RECREATION	specialist: ornithology fishing generalist: stroll/walk	1. Travel Cost/method 2. User Enjoyment/Visit 3. User willingness to Pay
EDUCATION	specialist: projects generalist: school visits	
RESEARCH	baseline monitoring including past history	Incalcuable
NON-USER		
EXISTENCE/BEQUEST	ecological 'role' existence for own sake options for future use bequest for future generations.	Incalculable/Indirect Non-user willingness to pay

spawning grounds for fish caught in another area or even by another country. Therefore there will clearly be an 'unknown' element in any attempt at valuation of such functions. The same may also be true of the value of the environment in disposing of waste products. It may be possible to calculate the cost of disposal by alternative means, in the event of biological systems having become so polluted that they can no longer absorb wastes, but an element of unknown 'cost' in environmental terms should still be acknowledged even though it cannot be measured. Protective functions afforded by direct sheltering of other habitats or human developments, as in the case of a sand dune system which acts as a first line of defence against flooding, may be valued indirectly by conventional means used to measure the costs of flooding or erosion which would result from the absence of such protection. A similar approach could be adopted to indirect protective functions, such as in the case where cliffs provide a sediment source which contributes to protection at another location.

Measurement of functions in the user category depend largely on the application of Contingent Valuation Methods (CVM) for allocating monetary values. Functions such as recreation and educational use of a site may be valued by the Travel Cost Method (TCM) which uses journey costs as substitute values for measuring willingness to pay for the recreational or educational experience (Stabler and Ash 1978). However, there are several limitations apparent when attempting to apply this approach to the valuation of recreational benefit at the coast in Britain, where the journey itself may be part of the recreational experience and may not take the most direct route to the location under study. Additionally, recreational activities are often complex, incorporating more than one activity in the same trip and being combined with other activities, such as shopping or visiting relatives, which may not be considered as recreational in nature.

An alternative approach is the use of questionnaires to assess Enjoyment per Visit by comparison with recreational activities with a known cost attached which will provide comparable enjoyment value (Penning-Rowsell et al. 1989). The application of this method to valuing recreational enjoyment of coastal sites will be outlined in the second part of this paper. This approach could also be applied to valuing educational use although its function as a surrogate valuation technique should be stressed since it would in no way seek to measure the 'total educational value' gained from the visit.

Willingness to Pay in money terms is another CVM approach which may be employed to measure user values and this is particularly appropriate in the case of specialist user activities carried out at a specific site, for example, bird-watching at a nature reserve. The direct willingness to pay for entry to or use of the facility or site may be taken as a measure of its value to the user. Indirect willingness to pay, e.g. through the taxation system, for upkeep of the environment in general, such as Heritage Coasts, may also be measured by the use of questionnaires assessing willingness to pay (Green, Tunstall and House 1989).

Putting a value on the research function of the environment is a far more problematic area to tackle and it may be seen as occupying a 'grey area' between the 'User' and 'Intrinsic' categories. Research is clearly an important component of environmental value which may be of direct use to society, for example, as a baseline against which change can be monitored and as a knowledge base on which predictions can be made. It may also be considered as becoming part of the past history of a site itself and, other things being equal (which they rarely are!), to lose a site with a recorded history could be considered a greater loss than to lose one without. This component of value clearly overlaps with both the concepts of educational and historical value.

The components considered so far constitute all the ways in which we, both as a society and as individuals within that society, make use of the environment in a direct or an indirect manner. In contrast, the third category contains other things about the environment apart from its use which we know are valued by some people. Although the term 'Intrinsic' has been adopted for this non-use category, we have to recognise that these components also reflect the values which we as humans put on the environment. One way of putting a money value on these components is through non-user willingness to pay, obtained in the same way as for user willingness to pay, although there is an obvious methodological difficulty here in that the sample population is the whole of society and not a specifically defined user group. Existence, option and bequest values may all be assessed using this approach. Existence value represents the value of something for its own sake now and in the future, independent of any use or recreational benefit which society or individuals would gain from that existence. The most familiar example of assessing this type of value is by asking for the amount of money individuals are willing to pay to ensure the continued existence of the Blue Whale. Perhaps this concept of value is the nearest thing to a genuine intrinsic value, even though we as humans are making a value judgement by saying that something has a right to exist and that by taking away its right to existence we are diminishing our own standing as humans (Brennan 1988).

Option value may be easier to conceptualise since it relates to the price individuals are willing to pay in order to keep their options open to some future point in time when they may want access to the environmental component. Bequest value can be considered as an extension of this to willingness to pay for keeping options open for future generations by handing on the environment in the same condition in which it has come to us, if not in a better one!

When we turn to the possibility of valuing the ecological 'role' or systemic value of the environment, then the technique of assessing willingness to pay is a very inadequate vehicle for allocating monetary value. Since the concept of ecological role relates ultimately to maintaining the environmental integrity of the global ecosystem, we may consider this of incalculable value since it is beyond price.

Aside from consideration of ecological role, several attempts have been made to find indirect measures of how both individuals and society as a whole value the other components of intrinsic value. Willis and Benson (1988) found out how much individuals would be willing to pay to view the haymeadows of the Yorkshire Dales both by direct willingness to pay and through the travel cost method. But arguably such measures relate more to the general amenity value or aesthetic value of the meadows, e.g. as the setting for a picnic, than to any component of 'intrinsic worth'. This view is supported by the fact that only the user population was questioned – we have no values from the non-users. And even if these meadows did not have attractive flowers and were not suitable locations for walks or picnics, would this mean that they had no value to society? If they appear to have no value at present, this does not allow for the concept of bequest value to future generations.

A previous paper has already discussed the problems of distinguishing between society's values and the aggregate values of individuals within that society. An alternative approach to estimation of the value which society puts on some component of the environment is therefore given by taking as surrogate values the cost to the nation of compensating farmers and land owners for profits foregone, through the environmentally sensitive management of designated areas under management agreements. However, we need to recognise that such a value is wholly an artifact of the agricultural economy at a particular point in time. A second approach to social valuation is to take the value which statutory or voluntary agencies have paid to aquire a site in order to protect it. But this value is also an artifact of market conditions at one point in time and, as such, may grossly distort our attempts to gain a realistic measure of intrinsic environmental value. Hence it is not surprising that in general we tend to put values or surrogate values on those things which are most easily measured and not necessarily those which are most important.

Application of survey-based valuation methods

The remaining sections of this paper focus on the experience of the Flood Hazard Research Centre in applying two methods, the Contingent Valuation Method (CVM) and the Travel Cost Method (TCM), to value the benefits that people obtain from using environmental resources for recreation: recreation benefits. As Colin Green has indicated in his paper, our experience gives us some confidence that it is possible to obtain reliable and valid valuations of recreation benefits, but non-use benefits remain altogether a more difficult issue to resolve.

The Travel Cost Method is perhaps the most widely accepted and used method for evaluating recreational benefits. Developed by Clawson in the United States in 1959, it has been extensively reviewed and used both in Britain and in the US (Clawson 1959; Harrison and Stabler 1981; Rosenthal, Loomis and Petersen 1984; Duffield 1984; Green et al. 1990a).

The method does not have to be based upon a survey; one of the advantages of the method is that it does not require extensive information to apply it. Straightforward visitor statistics on the number and origins of visitors and on the populations of areas of origin are sufficient. However, information on the origins of site users is often obtained through visitors' surveys. The TCM is an indirect method, in which the costs associated with travelling to a site are taken as a proxy for the value of the visit. Some of the limitations of this approach have already been mentioned. The method is obviously most appropriate where recreation benefits accrue to visitors who travel to reach the site rather than to sites which have mainly local users who do not travel. Coastal recreation would appear to be an appropriate application for the method since many visitors on the coast are on day trips travelling from some distance away. Since travel costs will depend in part on the distance travelled, a basic assumption of the method is that the value of the enjoyment of a visit must be higher for those who travel further and thus incur greater travel costs. This assumption has been tested in surveys of beach users carried out at ten sites in 1988 and 1989 as part of the Coastal Protection Research Project which the Centre has undertaken for the Ministry of Agriculture, Fisheries and Food (Figure 6.2). The value of the enjoyment of a visit to the beach was measured by asking visitors, using the CVM. The value of the visit was also estimated using the TCM: visitors' travel costs were estimated using the AUTOROUTE programme to compute the quickest route, the shortest distance and the cheapest cost of travel between the place of origin and the site for day visitors. It was found that there was a positive relationship between the travel costs involved and the value put on the enjoyment of the day's visit at only two sites, Spurn Head and Dunwich, both undeveloped sites rather than resorts, out of ten sites. The same was true of travel time and distance at the sites surveyed in 1988. It was concluded, therefore, that the TCM cannot generally be advised as a means of valuing coastal recreational benefits and that its use in any other context would need to be validated using survey data.

The two methods, the TCM and CVM, measure different things. The

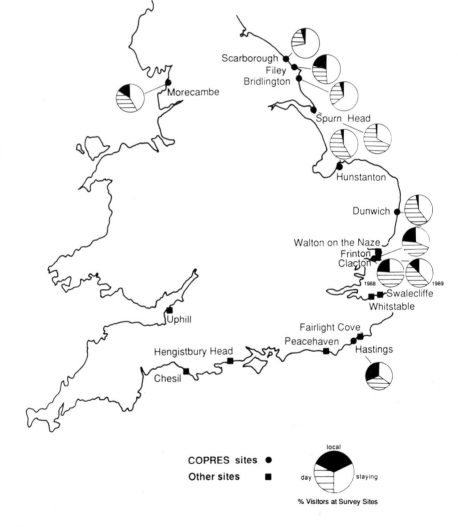

Figure 6.2   Coastal protection research project: 1988 and 1989

TCM measures the expectation of enjoyment of a visit before the visit takes place, since the visitor has to commit himself to incur the travel costs at that point. The Contingent Valuation Method is applied during the course of the visit and measures the enjoyment of the visit as it is experienced. The two methods are only likely to yield the same results if visitors set out with a clear intention of visiting a specific site, are familiar with the site and are able accurately to judge the enjoyment a visit to a particular destination will give them before setting out. These are assumptions about visiting behaviour that need to be tested if the method is to be applied (Green et al. 1990a, 1990b).

The CVM or expressed preference approach is a direct rather than indirect valuation method. It is essentially a survey-based method in which individuals, in a structured way in carefully designed survey questions, are asked about their personal valuations of increases or decreases in the availability of a good: a beach site or river corridor for example.

The method has been developed and tested by resource and environmental economists in the United States since the early 1960s. In the last 20 years in the United States, the method has been used in valuing a wide range of environmental goods and has been the subject of methodological research funded by the United States Environmental Protection Agency (Desvousges et al. 1983; Cummings, Brookshire and Schulze 1986; Mitchell and Carson 1989). The method has been recommended by the US Water Resources Council (1979) as a preferred method for valuing outdoor recreation benefits in benefit cost analyses. In addition, CVM has been recommended by the US Department of the Interior (1986) for valuing natural resource damages.

Although acceptance and use of the method is not as well established in Britain as in the United States, a substantial number of CVM studies have now been undertaken in Britain, the majority of them for government departments or as part of government financed contracts, but as yet there has been no major methodological research in Britain to test the method (Tunstall, Green and Lord, 1988: Green et al. 1990a). Some recent Flood Hazard Research Centre applications of the CVM in valuing recreation benefits are shown in Table 6.1. In a survey in Maidenhead, Berkshire, local residents were asked to put a value on environmental improvements to an existing flood relief channel, improvements such as increasing the flow of water in the channel and new planting in and near the channel (Coker, Tunstall and Penning-Rowsell 1989). Surveys involving over 800 river corridor users were carried out at 12 sites, country parks, town parks and town centres in different parts of England as part of a Department of the

Table 6.1 Comparison of values of enjoyment of visit obtained in different surveys (£ per adult visit).

DATE OF SURVEY	1989	1988	1988	1987	1987
Sample	Beach users – 4 sites	Beach users – 6 sites	Beach users – Hastings	Maidenhead residents	River corridor users – 12 sites
Goods valued	Beach now	Beach now	Beach now	River corridor improvements to Maidenhead Ditch	Water quality improvements
Mean	7.55	7.75	7.72	0.94	0.51
Log Mean	0.70	0.74	0.70	−0.25	−0.23
Log std deviation	0.40	0.37	0.42	0.39	0.38
Number of cases	603	737	198	242	837

Environment funded study of the social costs of sewerage. River corridor users were asked to value improvements in river water quality (Green, Tunstall and House 1989).

Much of the CVM research carried out at the Centre has been concerned with valuing coastal recreation. In the summers of 1988 and 1989 as part of the Coastal Protection Research Project financed by the Ministry of Agriculture, Fisheries and Food, surveys were conducted at ten coastal sites, both resorts and undeveloped sites in England (Figure 6.2). Valuations of beach recreation were obtained in the surveys from adults using the beach or promenade for recreation. The recreation value of clifftops has also been investigated in a survey of cliff-top users at the Naze, Essex (Penning-Rowsell et al. 1989), and in a survey of residents in Peacehaven, Sussex. A CVM survey of households and seafront users was carried out at Herne Bay for Canterbury City Council in the summer of 1990 to examine the value placed on major improvements to the seafront involving an off-shore reef.

Problems and issues in applying the CVM

There are two main issues that have to be addressed in applying the CVM:

- first, the issue of defining and representing the environmental resource or change to be valued to the respondents in the survey;
- second, the problem of developing reliable and valid measures of the value placed on the resource or change for use in the survey.

Defining the environmental good or change

A major advantage of the CVM compared with the TCM is that it can be used to value not only the current availability of an environmental or recreational good but also to obtain valuations under varying hypothetical conditions or changes. The TCM can only give valuations for the current situation. But in order to take advantage of this strength, first, it is necessary to be able to predict the changes that may occur so that realistic CVM scenarios can be presented to the respondents in the survey. There is often considerable uncertainty over the likely environmental changes. These are often complex. For example, it is frequently difficult to know exactly how a beach profile and composition may be affected by continuing erosion. Thus, any

Table 6.2 Factors important in the choice of recreational site to visit (mean rating) in 1988 beach surveys.

	Clacton	Scarboro'	Frinton	Filey	Dunwich	Spurn Hd
I wanted to visit the coast	8.5 (1)	8.1 (1)	6.3	8.2 (1)	8.5 (1)	7.0 (3)
The promenade/dunes/cliff is good for walking on	7.6 (2)	6.2	6.1	6.6	4.0	6.7 (5)
The beach is clean	7.3 (3)	7.8 (3)	6.7 (1)	8.0 (2)	7.0 (5)	5.5
The ease of access from home	7.2 (4)	5.7	5.6	5.9	6.0	4.1
The quietness	6.8 (5)	4.4	6.6 (2)	7.1	7.9 (3)	8.1 (1)
The type of beach (i.e. sand, pebbles, etc.)	6.0	7.9 (2)	6.5 (3)	7.8 (3)	2.0	5.0
The beach is good for children	5.0	7.5 (4)	4.9	6.9	3.2	4.5
I have liked it when I have been before	6.5	7.5 (4)	6.4 (4)	6.0	6.2	5.2
The attractive, natural setting of the beach	6.6	7.0	6.4 (4)	7.3 (5)	8.3 (2)	7.2 (2)
The spaciousness of the beach	6.0	7.4	6.1	7.7 (4)	7.2 (4)	6.2
The beach is good for walks	0.5	6.3	5.3	7.1	5.0	6.8 (4)

(i) Scale is from 10 (very important to my choice) to 0 (not at all important to my choice).
(ii) Most important five factors shown from each site are indicated in brackets.

representation of a good or a change in a survey is likely to involve making assumptions and simplifications.

Second, it necessary to establish that the public which uses the resource can discriminate and recognise the changes under investigation. Thus, since little was known about preferences for and perceptions of beaches, the 1988 beach surveys were used to gain insights into public perceptions and preferences. At the most basic level, data was obtained on the importance of beach and seafront characteristics in the visitor's choice to visit a particular site. The results are shown in Table 6.2. The research also examined the way in which the physical characteristics of the beach affected the kind of recreational activities undertaken and the potential effects of specific erosive changes on enjoyment of coastal recreation and frequency of visiting (Penning-Rowsell et al. 1989)

Third, it is necessary to represent the good or changes accurately and in sufficient detail and to describe them to those you interview in a way that is clear and meaningful to them. For some environmental goods or resources, there may be an issue as to whether respondents are sufficiently familiar or informed about the subject to make valuation possible. The economic theory upon which the CVM is modelled assumes perfect knowledge of the good, the circumstances in which it is being supplied and the alternatives available. Therefore there is an argument for providing very full information about the good or change to be valued. But, in practical terms, there are limits to the amount of information that can be conveyed in a questionnaire, especially one being administered on a windy beach or river bank.

In investigating the value to residents of various enhancements to a flood relief channel and in examining the impact of coastal erosion upon recreational enjoyment and use of beaches and cliff tops, we used drawings combined with descriptive scenarios read out to respondents to represent the coast under varying conditions. An example of one set of drawings is shown in Figure 6.3. The scenario describing the beach at Morecambe after increased erosion was as follows:

- compared with Drawing A (showing the beach in current condition) there is no beach above high tide;
- the drop from the promenade to the beach is longer so the flights of steps are longer;
- at low tide there is no sand and the beach is mostly mud with a narrow band of shingle at the top;
- there are no groynes along this section of the beach;
- the seawall is in poor condition, with cracks and holes and the sea is washing in underneath.

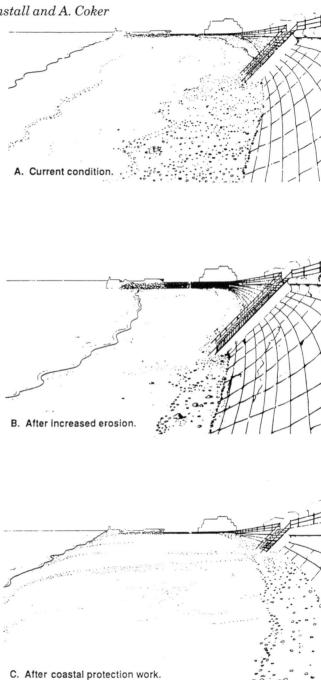

Figure 6.3 Drawings of same section of beach under different conditions (Morecombe, Lancashire).

This illustrates the difficulty of capturing a recreational resource – which is experienced with five senses – in words and schematic drawings, and the simplification and assumptions that have to be made in presenting CVM scenarios.

There is evidence in the CVM research literature, too, that the amount and kind of information provided to respondents in a CVM survey may affect their response to valuation questions (Burness et al. 1983; Samples, Dixon and Gowan 1986) and this has been described in the literature as 'information bias'. It is probably wrong to view this as a bias: rather, it should be recognised that contingent valuations will only be valid for the environmental good as defined and specified in the survey, because other definitions and specifications might yield different results.

Asking valuation questions in surveys

Several different methods of eliciting contingent valuations in surveys have been developed. Among the methods used are:

- a direct open question on the worth of a good or on willingness to pay for one;
- a payment card method in which respondents are presented with a card showing an array of possible values to chose from;
- an iterative bidding procedure in which respondents are repeatedly asked whether they value the good at more or less than a given sum;
- a fixed price closed question in which respondents have to say 'yes' or 'no' to an offered price for a good.

Researchers recognise that people are unaccustomed to placing a value on unpriced goods and find valuation questions difficult to answer. The various questioning procedures aim to ensure that respondents consider well and make the necessary effort to arrive at a valuation. As with any survey question, there is evidence that the form of the valuation question and, particularly, that offering a starting value for respondents to consider, can affect the responses (Desvousges, Smith and McGivney 1983; Cummings, Brookshire and Schulze 1986).

Two different approaches have been adopted in Flood Hazard Research Centre Research using the CVM: first, the value of enjoyment per adult visit approach; second, willingness to pay through rates, taxes and water rates approach.

The value of enjoyment per adult visit
This approach was employed in the surveys of recreational users of river corridors, of beaches, promenades and clifftops and at Maidenhead. A simple direct open question was used to obtain valuations of the recreation experience, for example, in the beach surveys: 'What value do you put on your individual enjoyment of this visit to the beach today?'

To help respondents arrive at a valuation, they were asked to think of a visit or activity in which they had participated, which had given them the same amount of enjoyment as their visit to the beach today – they were shown a list of possible activities or visits including a country house or park, a leisure centre and a café, pub or restaurant, to set them thinking about the value of their beach recreation. It was suggested to respondents that they should use the costs of the alternative visit as a guide to the value of their beach recreation.

In the 1989 beach surveys, having given a valuation for today's visit, respondents were asked to consider the drawings of the beach in varying conditions (Figure 6.3) and to say whether they would get more or less enjoyment from a visit to the beach in the drawings compared to their enjoyment of today's visit and whether they would visit the beach in the drawing more or less often. They were then asked to value their enjoyment of a visit to the beach as shown in the drawings (Table 6.4).

Table 6.3   Value of 'today's' visit – from the 1988 and 1989 beach surveys.

		% able to value	Mean (£ per visit)	Log mean	Log std. dev.	Number of cases
1988						
	Filey	87	3.60	0.47	0.29	88
	Scarborough	83	5.00	0.57	0.35	101
	Spurn Head	80	8.50	0.83	0.29	97
	Hastings	66	7.70	0.70	0.42	247
	Dunwich	61	6.90	0.59	0.48	101
	Frinton	70	9.50	0.86	0.32	178
	Clacton	90	9.90	0.89	0.33	170
1989						
	Morecambe	92	5.80	0.56	0.42	150
	Bridlington	86	5.90	0.64	0.36	151
	Hunstanton	90	8.70	0.81	0.36	152
	Clacton	67	10.50	0.85	0.40	146

Table 6.4   Value of enjoyment of visit by visitor type (£ per adult visit)

All sites 1989 Beach surveys	Visitor type			
	Local	Day	Staying	All
	Mean £ per visit	Mean £ per visit	Mean £ per visit	Mean £ per visit
Today's visit	5.70	8.10	7.50	7.60
Beach in current state (Drawing A)	5.60	7.60	7.00	7.10
Beach after erosion (Drawing B)	3.10	4.30	3.30	3.70
Beach after protection (Drawing C)	6.50	9.70	9.30	9.20

Having followed this procedure, over 80% were able to value today's visit (mean 80% in 1988 surveys and 84% in 1989; the percentages for the individual sites are shown in Table 6.3) and in the 1989 beach surveys, most then went on to offer valuations of the beach as shown in the drawings. Some of the respondents unwilling to offer a valuation regarded their beach recreation very highly, in some cases as a unique experience, and stated that they could not value these things in money terms. Significant differences have been found in the value of enjoyment per visit offered by local, day and staying visitors in the beach recreation surveys (Table 6.4).

In order to estimate the economic losses associated with a deterioration in beach condition through erosion, it is necessary, first, to evaluate the change in the enjoyment per recreational visit that visitors experience: in our 1989 beach surveys, this is given by the difference in value of enjoyment of a visit to the beach in current condition (as shown in Drawing A) and to the beach after increased erosion (as shown in Drawing B). But the possibility that current visitors will transfer their visits elsewhere if the beach deteriorates must also be considered. Whether or not an economic loss is involved in the transfer of visits to alternative sites will depend on two factors: the value of the enjoyment visitors get from a visit to the alternative site and the value of any additional travel costs incurred. If visitors can go to another site which gives them as much enjoyment at no extra cost, ie there is a perfect substitute site for their recreation, then there will be no economic loss involved in the beach deterioration. In the 1989 beach surveys visitors were asked whether they would visit the eroded beach much less often, much more often or the same amount as now. If they said that they would visit less often they were asked where they would visit instead. The value of the enjoyment of a visit to the alternative site and any additional costs in travelling there were elicited. From these data it was possible to estimate economic losses associated with coastal erosion at the beach sites, taking into account both the changes in enjoyment of the recreation and transferred visits (Table 6.5).

Table 6.5   Economic losses to visitors from beach erosion

1989 Beach Surveys	Per cent who would move	Loss £ per adult visit	Log mean	Log standard deviation
Bridlington	59	3.46	0.38	0.41
Clacton	44	4.37	0.55	0.41
Hunstanton	67	3.43	0.52	0.36
Morecambe	65	3.34	0.41	0.44
Overall:				
Local visitors	43	1.58	0.38	0.36
Day visitors	61	2.37	0.47	0.40
Staying visitors	63	5.55	0.46	0.44

Willingness to pay questions

This approach has been used in Centre surveys mainly to value general environmental goods or changes such as coastal protection in England and Wales, or improved national river water quality rather than to value changes at specific sites. But in the cliff top survey at the Naze in Essex, and in a survey of residents at Peacehaven, Sussex, willingness to pay questions were used to elicit values for protecting the specific site (Penning-Rowsell et al. 1989).

Willingness to pay questions usually involve specifying a mechanism by which payment is to be made: rates and taxes, water rates, entrance fees, a special fund or higher prices. There is some evidence that the responses to willingness to pay questions are affected by the payment mechanism chosen and that valuations may reflect attitudes towards this mechanism as well as the value placed on the good itself (Tunstall, Green and Lord 1988). It is easy to imagine that this would have been the case if the 'poll tax' had been used as a payment mechanism in 1990. It can be argued, however, that since coastal protection, river water pollution abatement and other environmental changes are financed through mechanisms such as rates and taxes, that it is realistic and appropriate to specify them in valuation questions.

Centre surveys eliciting willingness to pay valuations have sought to obtain realistic and conservative valuations by presenting respondents with information, for example, on current national expenditure on the coastal protection or river water pollution abatement, by reminding respondents of other areas of public expenditure on which they might prefer money to be spent and by stating that in current circumstances respondents may not be able to afford to pay more in order to legitimate

Table 6.6   Willingness to pay for coastal protection in £ per year by visitor type

1989 Beach Surveys	Local	Day	Staying	All
% willing to pay	53	69	69	68
Mean £ per person:				
Starting point 50p	2.02	6.50	3.68	4.90
Starting point £2.50	6.54	6.45	8.28	7.22
Log mean £ per person:				
Starting point 50p	0.03	0.21	0.14	0.16
Starting point £2.50	0.57	0.53	0.66	0.59

a 'no' response to the willingness to pay questions. More than half the respondents have usually been willing to pay in our applications of this CVM approach. The proportion has usually been higher for coastal protection (Penning-Rowsell et al. 1989). Willingness to pay extra in rates and taxes for coastal protection was obtained in the 1989 beach surveys using a bidding procedure with two starting points and the results indicate that starting point bias may be present (Table 6.6).

The value of the enjoyment of a visit approach and willingness to pay questions measure different things. The value of the enjoyment of a visit questions aim to elicit recreational user values only, whereas the willingness to pay valuations not only include the value associated with the use of the resource but also a range of possible non-use values which are considered in Colin Green's paper. Furthermore, it can be argued that values obtained using the value per visit method are less likely to be constrained by income than are willingness to pay valuations. The nature of this constraint on willingness to pay is also examined in Colin Green's paper.

In common with other CVM researchers and for pragmatic reasons, the research carried out at the Centre has employed questions which sought willingness to pay to prevent deterioration or achieve an improvement rather than a form of questioning in which the individual's willingness to accept compensation for a deterioration or for doing without an improvement are elicited. A number of studies have shown that the latter method yields higher valuations than the former, whereas economic theory would lead us to expect the methods to achieve similar results (Tunstall, Green and Lord 1988). It can be argued that where a potential deterioration or loss has to be valued, the willingness to accept compensation would be the more appropriate form.

The reliability and validity of CVM valuations

True tests of the reliability of contingent valuations are rare since ideally they require that a survey is repeated after an interval of time with the same individuals using the same valuation questions. The few tests that have been carried out have shown respondents to be consistent in their responses over time (Jones-Lee, Hammerton and Philips 1985; Mitchell and Carson 1989). It has not been possible to mount a test of the reliability of contingent valuations as part of Centre research but a survey of beach and promenade users was carried out at the same site, Clacton, in both 1988 and 1989, using the same questioning procedure but with different samples of users. There were no significant differences in the mean valuations obtained in the two years at Clacton. Indeed, if differences in the value of money are taken into account, the results would have been even closer (Table 6.3).

Direct validation of contingent valuations – a comparison of hypothetical with actual payments – has rarely been possible and where it has been tested the subjects of the valuation have been closer to marketed good than the typical subjects of a contingent valuation survey. Although some experiments have reported differences between actual and hypothetical payments, the evidence is not conclusive and researchers are divided in their interpretation of the evidence (Tunstall, Green and Lord 1988).

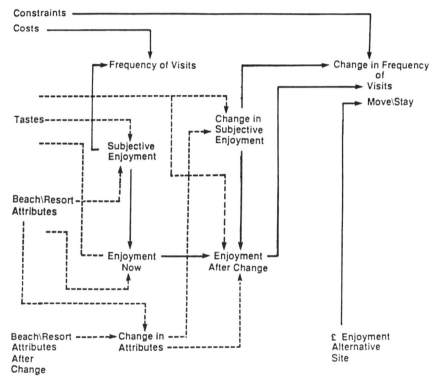

Key

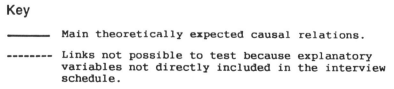

———— Main theoretically expected causal relations.

-------- Links not possible to test because explanatory variables not directly included in the interview schedule.

Figure 6.4   Theoretical model underlying 1989 beach survey

Another approach to validation is to compare the results of contingent valuations with the valuations obtained by indirect methods such as the travel cost method (Tunstall, Green and Lord 1988). However, our research on coastal recreation leads us to question the assumptions of the travel cost method and therefore its usefulness as a test of the validity of contingent valuations.

In our research using the CVM, a similar questioning technique has been used to obtain valuations of different resources in different settings. The method has yielded different results in valuing different things: the enjoyment of a visit with improvements in river water quality and the enjoyment of a visit to a beach (Table 6.2). When the mean values for the enjoyment of today's visit obtained at different coastal sites are compared, significant differences are found between, for example, Clacton and Bridlington and the other two sites included in the 1989 survey (Table 6.3). The measurement method, therefore, appears to discriminate and this indicates that the method has discriminant validity.

Finally, CVM surveys need to be based on a theoretical model of the recreation behaviour under investigation. Figure 6.4 presents the underlying theoretical model for the 1989 beach surveys. Validity tests can then be built into the questionnaire and the relationships between the variables in the model, particularly the contingent valuation and other variables, can be examined in the analysis to see whether the predicted relationships hold indicating construct validity. Some preliminary analyses of this kind were carried out on the 1989 beach recreation surveys for local visitors (Green et al. 1990b). We have argued that the great advantage of the CVM is that such tests of the validity of the method can be incorporated into the surveys (Tunstall, Green and Lord 1988).

The results that we have obtained using the CVM give us some grounds for increasing confidence in the reliability and validity of the method and therefore lead us to suggest that this is a method which can be utilised for putting monetary values on intangibles such as recreational enjoyment which were, until recently, considered outside the scope of economic evaluation.

References

Brennan, A. (1988) *Thinking about Nature*, Routledge.
Burness, H. S., Cummings, R. G., Mehr, A. F. and Walpert, M. S. (1983) Valuing policies which reduce environmental risk, *Natural Resources Journal* 23(3), 675–82.

Clawson, M. (1959) *Methods for measuring the demand for outdoor recreation*, Reprint No. 10, Washington DC: Resources for the Future.

Coker, A., Tunstall, S. M. and Penning-Rowsell, E. C. (1989) *An Evaluation of the Recreation and Amenity benefits of a Flood Alleviation Scheme for Maidenhead*, Enfield: Flood Hazard Research Centre.

Cummings, R. R., Brookshire, D. S. and Schulze, W. D. (1986) *Valuing Environmental Goods: an Assessment of the 'Contingent Valuation Method'*, Totowa: Rowman & Allanheld.

Desvousges, W. H., Smith, V. K. and McGivney, M. P. (1983) *A comparison of alternative approaches for estimating recreation and related benefits of water quality improvement*, Washington DC: Office of Policy Analysis, US Environmental Protection Agency.

Duffield, J. (1984) Travel costs and contingent valuation: a comparative analysis, *Advances in applied micro-economics* 3, 67–87.

Green, C. H., Tunstall, S. M. and House, M. A. (1989) Evaluating the benefits of river water quality improvement, in van der Staal, P. M. and van Vught, F. A. (eds) *Impact forecasting and assessment: methods, results, experiences*, Delft: Delft University Press, 171–80.

Green, C. H., Tunstall, S. M., N'Jai, A. and Rogers, A. (1990a) Economic evaluation of environmental goods, *Project Appraisal* (5)2, 70–82.

Green, C. H., Tunstall, S. M., Penning-Rowsell, E. P. and Coker, A. (1990b) *The benefits of coast protection: results from testing the Contingent Valuation Method for valuing beach recreation*, paper presented to the conference of River and Coastal Engineers, Loughborough University, England.

Harrison, A. J. M. and Stabler, M. J. (1981) An analysis of journeys for canal-based recreation, *Regional Studies* 15(5), 345–58.

Jones-Lee, M. W., Hammerton, M. and Philips, P. R. (1985) The value of safety: results of a national sample survey, *Economics Journal* 95, 49–72.

Mitchell, R. C. and Carson, R. T. (1989) *Using surveys to value public goods: the contingent valuation method*, Washington: Resources for the future.

Penning-Rowsell, E. C., Coker, A., N'Jai, A., Parker, D. J. and Tunstall, S. M. (1989) Scheme Worthwhileness, *Coastal Management: proceedings of the conference organized by the Institution of Civil Engineers and held in Bournemouth on 9–11 May 1989*, 227–41. London: Thomas Telford.

Rosenthal, D. H., Loomis, J. B. and Petersen, G.L. (1984) *The Travel Cost model: Concepts and Applications*, USDA Forest Service General Technical Report RM-109, Fort Collins: Rocky Mountain Forest and Range Experimental Station.

Samples, K. C., Dixon, J.A. and Gowan, M. M. (1986) Information disclosure and endangered species valuation, *Land Economics* 62, 306–12.

Stabler, M. J. and Ash, S. (1978) *The amenity demand for inland waterways: informal activities*, Reading: Amenity Waterways Study Unit, Department of Economics, University of Reading.

Tunstall, S. M., Green, C. H. and Lord, J. (1988) *The Evaluation of Environmental Goods by the Contingent Valuation Method*, Enfield: Flood Hazard Research Centre.

US Department of the Interior (1986) Natural resources damage assessments: Final rule, *Federal Register* 51 (148), 27674–753, Washington DC: US Government Printing Office.

US Water Resources Council (1979) Procedures for evaluation of National Economic Development (NED): benefits and costs in water planning (level C), Final rule, *Federal Register* (14 December 1979) 44 (242), Washington DC: US Government Printing Office.

Willis, K. G. and Benson, J. F. (1988) A comparison of user benefits and costs of nature consrvation at three nature reserves, *Regional Studies* 22, 5.

6 Commentary

The application of Contingent Valuation Methods to informal recreation is fairly recent in Britain and there are several concerns about detailed issues of methodology. Beach and promenade recreation were studied in the surveys outlined in Chapter 6 as they are the major recreational uses of the coast in terms of numbers of users. In addition, beaches are important because they represent the first line of defence of the coast. Hence the majority of coast-protection work in this country is carried out on groynes and on stabilisation of promenades to prevent property falling into the sea.

The first issue of concern is the overall appropriateness of the methodology for putting a value on recreational enjoyment, and the reliability of the results. The research outlined in the previous chapter showed that the reliability of the method has been checked by statistical testing of the data to see if willingness-to-pay (WTP) is explicable in terms of other responses given in the questionnaire survey, and to see if internally consistent responses are made. At the same time it is possible to test the validity of the underlying theory, termed 'construct validity'. If the results are not consistent with the underlying theory, then either the measurement method or the theory is wrong. However, the results of the coasts surveys are largely consistent and therefore reproducible. It is generally possible to explain up to 40 per cent of the variance in the data between the differences in people's willingness to pay by way of hypothesised explanatory variables. Many regression analyses on Contingency Valuation Method (CVM) studies have less than 20 per cent explained variance, and it is unlikely that a value as great as 60 per cent will or can be reached in this type of survey. Within the theoretical model underlying the 1989 Beach Survey (Figure 6.4) for example, income would be one of the main constraints on willingness to pay. It is assumed that people are rational, but in fact it is found that about 6 per cent of respondents could get more enjoyment at less cost by visiting an alternative site to that which they did in fact visit. However, this may be explained as rational behaviour in relation to the purpose of the visit: for example, visiting relatives or the discovery when they visited the site that it did not live up to expectations. In order to cover as many possibilities as possible, the questions have been designed to be as detailed and wide-ranging as possible.

A second point of concern with the method involves the identification of boundaries of the study area. One problem is that if visitors to one beach choose, after erosion, to visit another site instead, then this could lead to congestion at that other site which might be outside the initial study area. The knock-on effects of seafront deterioration on the recreational enjoyment of users at another site might not therefore be incorporated into the evaluation process since existing users of that other site would potentially experience a loss of enjoyment due to the increase in congestion. Because of the need to draw initial boundaries to the study area, this presents problems and although, in principle, the knock-on effects should be considered, there are practical difficulties in doing so.

Another issue relates to the way in which zero values are handled in the analysis of willingness-to-pay data. CVM researchers have adopted a variety of approaches to the treatment of zero values. The questionnaires used by FHRC surveys first ask respondents whether they are willing to pay anything and then asks those who are willing to pay something how much they are willing to pay. This gives two sets of explanatory variables: a binary variable and a continuous variable respectively. In general around 50 per cent are not willing to pay anything. In the FHRC surveys a statement is read to the respondent before the question itself is asked, to legitimate their being unwilling to pay. Interviewees are told that there might be more important things than coast protection on which to spend money, such as the health service, or that they might not be able to afford extra expenditure. They are also generally given the current mean annual per capita expenditure on coast protection on a national basis. Consequently there is no pressure on respondents to give a positive answer. If people are willing to pay and give an amount, then other questions which could explain the differences in the values given are examined by regression analysis. If people are not willing to pay then possible reasons for this are examined by discriminant analysis. Total willingness to pay of the population can then be estimated as the proportion of respondents willing to pay multiplied by mean values given by those who are willing to pay.

A final point of concern over the method is with the degree of precision of the valuation target. There may be doubts about whether it is possible to separate the value of that part of the visit which is to the beach from other elements of a trip, for example to the town or other attraction. The way in which the method handles this is to consider the change in value of enjoyment after increased erosion and not the gross value of the visit. This is done by asking a wide range of questions in order to consider as many aspects of recreational user's behaviour as possible.

Arising from this, the overall benefits of the method in comparison with the Travel Cost Method (TCM) have to be weighed up. The use of TCM, which assumes that in theory there should be more enjoyment the greater the distance travelled (a 'gravity' model), has sometimes been found to be invalid in Britain. In the United States the situation may be different but, where distances are shorter and there are many substitute sites, this model of recreational behaviour cannot be shown to underlie actual behaviour. An exception to this was found by research at Spurn Head, although this may be explained by its location which necessitates visits being planned rather than casual. Its specialist geomorphological interest may also influence the patterns of visits.

It is important to emphasise that conclusions reached through the use of Contingent Valuation Methods consist of more than a simple numerical analysis of responses to willingness to pay questions. A framework of questions which can help to explain the behaviour of individuals is necessary and the method is continually being refined. That the results are likely to be valid is shown by data from several surveys of recreational users of coasts which produced consistent figures. Although many people have reservations about the use of CVM, as the methodology develops it does appear to provide a valid way in which to quantify recreational enjoyment.

7 Evaluating the environmental impact of coastal protection schemes

A. Coker

Any new development scheme at the coast which falls within the requirements for a statutory Environmental Impact Assessment is subject to the consultation procedure laid down in the DOE guide to the procedures of environmental assessment (1990). This procedure requires consultation with statutory environmental agencies at specific stages in the process of producing an impact statement.

However, most coast protection and sea defence schemes do not fall within the requirements of an environmental assessment. They are usually either too minor in scale to warrant an impact assessment, or, if they are schemes of a significant size, they normally involve the upgrading of an existing scheme rather than a new scheme, and therefore fall outside the requirements of the Statutory Instrument (1988). Nevertheless, the effects on the environment of both these types of scheme should be systematically considered in order to determine whether or not they will be significant.

Three main problems arise in this context; first, there may be inadequate environmental information available on which to base judgements about the likely impact of the proposed scheme. Second, whatever the environmental information available, it may not be presented in an appropriate form to enable the non-specialist to make meaningful comparisons of the likely effects of different courses of action. Third, the available information may not be contributed to the decision-making process at the most appropriate stage.

There are a number of individual measures which can be adopted to overcome these problems such as ensuring that all available information has been assembled, and providing a format in which the information can be clearly presented to facilitate the identification of impacts. But the most important measure is the establishment of a procedural framework within which the available environmental information can be fully utilised.

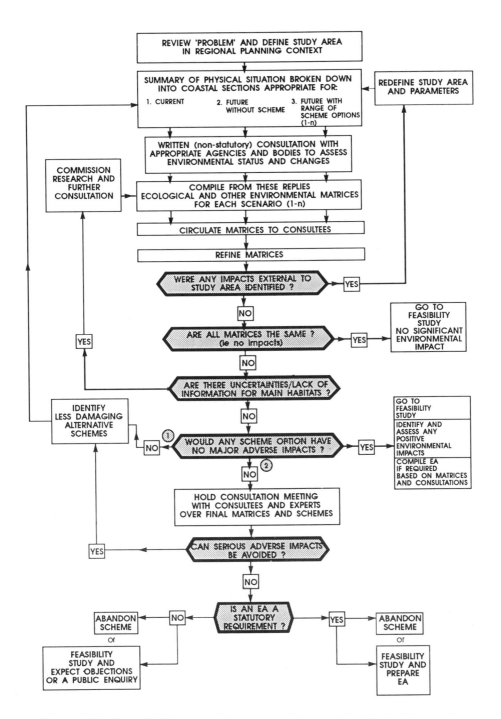

Figure 7.1 Consultation procedure on environmental effect of coastal protection schemes

Figure 7.1 outlines a consultation procedure which will enable the environmental inputs to be made at an early stage in the preparation of a scheme, thus enabling the possible effects on the environment of various courses of action to be adequately considered from the outset. It is necessary to stress that liaison should be established with all organisations who can advise on the prediction of the whole range of environmental impacts at the earliest stages of a pre-feasibility study. Not only is this likely to result in a more environmentally favourable solution but following this procedure should minimise objections by environmental interest groups which, almost inevitably, result in delays at a later stage in the scheme development. There is also the possibility that inadequate environmental information will exist on which to base evaluation of scheme effects, thus necessitating further information-gathering. The steps in the procedure are outlined below.

1.   The first step is the identification of the problem and definition of the study area. The procedure may be applied both to a scheme proposal at a specific location or in the context of the need to develop an area strategy at a regional or sub-regional scale. The nature of the problem and/or the scale of study area are first defined in engineering terms by the responsible Local Authority or National River Authority (NRA) region.

2.   Data and projections from an engineering survey will be required to summarise the physical characteristics of the coast. This information should be assembled under three headings:

   - the current situation – there may or may not be existing coast protection works in place modifying the natural characteristics of the coastline;
   - the future situation with *no* coastal protection scheme – there is likely to be continued environmental change by natural processes resulting in erosion/accretion/flooding. It should be noted that such changes may be considered desirable or undesirable depending on which environmental interest is being considered. Even within the ecological perspective, the same changes may be regarded differently from different points of view. For example, ornithologists may prefer the maintenance of current conditions which provide feeding grounds for particular bird species, whereas plant ecologists might welcome a radical change in the habitat which would allow the development of different successional plant communities;
   - the future situation – there may be a range of possible schemes and it will be necessary to predict the physical effects of the

proposed scheme or scheme options.

3. At this stage, and before proceeding further with outline scheme proposals in engineering terms, it is important to consult formally with all appropriate bodies, both statutory agencies and non-governmental organisations, who may have an interest in the area. It should not be assumed that the existing designation of an area is the only indicator of ecological importance since some interesting areas may fail to be designated for a variety of practical reasons. The fact that a site is not designated does not mean that it has no ecological value. The organisations consulted should be asked to assess the current status and importance of the area from their own perspective and to predict its possible vulnerability to change resulting from the various scheme proposals as well as from the 'do nothing' scenario.

4. The clearest way to summarise this potentially complex and diverse information is in the form of three, or more, environmental matrices for each of the components of environmental value, as illustrated in the example of Hengistbury Head (Figure 9.2). This should enable comparisons to be made so that the likely implications of various courses of action (or inaction) can be easily assessed and understood by the non-specialist. A set of environmental matrices should be compiled for each environmental component of the area under consideration, i.e. its ecology, archaeology, etc. The matrices should show both the magnitude of the change and its significance. This may be done either by in-house environmental expertise of the proposing agency or, more usually, by specialists in each field.

5. The next stage should highlight any areas of missing information which prevent the drawing up of the matrices. It is then necessary to consult more widely to ascertain whether such information exists or to commission further study to enable data-gathering from empirical sources, where absence of such information is potentially significant. Nevertheless it must be recognised that there will normally be various uncertainties associated with predicting impacts on ecological systems of changes in environmental conditions. It is never possible to have complete information on which to base predictions and a decision will have to be made about what constitutes an 'adequate' information base on which to proceed.

6. The matrices should then be circulated for comment and refinement among all relevant consultees.

7. Environmental advisors will also be able to indicate whether there are any impacts external to the study area as initially

defined, i.e. knock-on effects to other sites, for example as a result of reduction in sediment supply. If this is the case, it will then be necessary to redefine the physical parameters of the study area before proceeding further.

8. Next, the matrices should be compared to see whether or not there are any significant environmental impacts with the proposed scheme. The same questions should be asked of all environmental advisors in parallel concerning any relevant components of environmental interest, (e.g. archaeology, geology and ecology).

9. In the unlikely case of all matrices being the same (i.e. a scheme with no adverse environmental impacts), then the next stage is to proceed to a feasibility study of the scheme. Where environmental impacts occur of such a minor nature as to be judged unimportant, then the study can also proceed to the feasibility stage. This clearly raises the issue of what constitutes a significant or minor scheme impact and who should be responsible for making such judgements. This can only be resolved through negotiation with representatives of the appropriate interests in each individual case. A more likely situation would be that the matrices will show some environmental changes resulting from the scheme.

10. Where comparison of matrices shows uncertainty concerning prediction of change for any of the main habitats, the question of how to handle lack of information is raised. If the inadequacies of existing information are such as to make prediction of scheme effects impossible, the next step must be to carry out further environmental research such as ecological surveys. It is clear that the need for this should be identified early on in the process, to save delays at a later stage, especially where seasonal considerations constrain survey work. The scope and scale of such research will depend, in practice, on the scale of the coastal protection works proposed. The larger the scheme and the more extensive the area, the greater will be the necessary lead-in time for the scheme.

The stage indicated as 'further research' may involve no more than collecting together all the existing information about the area from all those agencies and organisations with data and observations to contribute. For example, in the case of Hengistbury Head, the timescale given by the Local Authority was such that two site visits, consultation with English Nature (EN), formerly the Nature Conservancy Council (NCC), the local wildlife Trust, a Natural History Society, a local ornithological group and the warden of the Local Nature Reserve were all that could be carried out. Predictions had to be made on the best informed estimates and from available secondary source descriptive material.

In a larger project or one where the ecological importance of the area was recognised at the outset, further research could involve more detailed investigations, primary fieldwork, predictive modelling of ecological impacts, etc. In any case, further investigation would enable the matrices to be completed in a more detailed way and ideally would ensure that predictions of change reflected the sum of best available information at that point in time.

11. With this more comprehensive information, it should then be possible to identify whether any scheme variant would be without major adverse impact. If so, a feasibility study of that specific scheme variant would follow. At that stage it is necessary to predict whether the scheme could also have any positive impacts, such as the creation of new habitats by altered deposition, and if so, to evaluate these changes as benefits of the scheme.

12. In the event of all proposed schemes having adverse impacts, it is important for environmentalists and engineers together to attempt to identify less damaging alternatives – either of the scheme overall or of ways of implementing the existing scheme proposals. If such an alternative can be identified, this would require the procedure to be followed through for a second time when, ideally, a scheme could be produced which would avoid any serious impacts. The main scheme feasibility study could then be undertaken with confidence that any environmental impacts had been fully recognised and taken into account at the outset.

13. A more complex situation arises where different scheme variants differ in their impacts on the various components of environmental value, which is normally the case. It may appear impossible to identify which is the least damaging scheme, in environmental terms, in the absence of a common numeraire. However, the solution proposed here is to sit down with the representatives of all the environmental interests concerned and, informed by the matrices, to attempt to reach a preferred solution through discussions and trade-offs. This process of trade-offs obviously becomes even more complex where the potential gains to one environmental component have to be weighed against the actual known losses to another. Ultimately, it is for politicians to decide the public acceptability of the trade-offs preferred by professional advisors in the final decision-making process.

14. Whichever scheme alternative is finally selected, if serious impacts to any component of environmental value appear to be unavoidable despite negotiation, and the coastal protection authority does not wish to abandon plans for a scheme, all that may be possible is to note the likelihood of contention over the scheme and the possible objections or need for a public enquiry before proceeding.

A consultation procedure such as this should meet the objectives of the need for a co-ordinated environmental input, in a summary form, easily comprehended by the non-specialist and at an early stage in the decision-making process. In the absence of an economic valuation or even a quantitative evaluation of relative impacts, it provides the mechanism for the implicit valuation of environmental resources through the decision-making process.

References

Department of the Environment and Welsh Office (1990) *Environmental Assessment: a guide to the procedures*, London: HMSO.

Department of the Environment (1988) Town and Country Planning (Assessment of Environmental Effects) Regulations (SI No 1199). London: HMSO.

7 Commentary

One way of viewing the procedure outlined in the previous chapter is to regard it as the formalisation of a process that already happens in many cases. There are obvious advantages in a more systematic process, particularly as it might avoid conflict at a later stage and provide the material for an Environmental Assessment (EA) if needed.

However, it is important to stress that the procedure is more than just a way of improving the consultation process. It is, in itself, a means by which decisions can be made without the need for quantification or valuation of environmental impacts. Within the process of trade-offs lies the mechanism for a more systematic form of decision-making based on implicit valuations of environmental resources.

The main problem with the procedure is that there is little immediate incentive for coast protection authorities to carry out an apparently complex non-statutory procedure, particularly where they do not have specialists to interpret the information collected, for example, in the ecological matrices. When the procedure becomes part of MAFF's requirements for grant aid submissions for coast protection schemes, then the process will be more easily accepted. A useful development would be to expand the role of the process, in strategic planning terms, by involving County Councils. Many are already developing a greater interest and role in coastal planning and might be able to provide staff and expertise to encourage wider integration in the use of the procedure.

Some points concerning application of the procedure should be emphasised; first, the procedure needs to be integrated with the existing planning process and legislation, hence it should identify from the outset where a statutory EA is likely to be required in the long run. One concern arising from this is the differing status of coast protection and sea defence. Since the latter comes under land drainage legislation the procedure needs to allow for this which should help to standardise the process in coastal engineering schemes. Second, it is important that the procedure is started prior to a Local Authority giving itself planning permission for a scheme. Since Local Authorities are usually the Coast Protection Authorities (CPAs) there is a danger that they will ignore the procedure, yet it is a way for them to improve their decisions and reduce conflict in the long term.

One advantage of the procedure which should be highlighted when persuading CPAs to adopt it is that the procedure effectively results in an Environmental Statement in advance of any statutory requirement, thereby minimising conflicts and unnecessary costs (such as full feasibility studies of contentious options).

It is important for the procedure to be set in a regional context. If the CPAs alone define the study area this may be too small to encompass all knock-on environmental effects thus necessitating delays in the process while the affected area is redefined and revised predictions and consultations are made – a waste of time for both CPA and consultees. If regional associations such as the Standing Conference on Problems Associated with the Coastline (SCOPAC) or County Councils are involved at an early stage in defining the study area then this would improve the scope of the process.

It is also important to consider as wide a range of feasible options as possible. One of the advantages of this procedure is in identifying at an early stage the trade-offs between scheme options with a wide range of environmental impacts on the ecological, archaeological and recreational components of an area. Parallel appraisal of the impacts of the various options on all components of the environment may lead to alternative options being put forward. The whole range of options could then be prioritised in terms of the extent of their individual impact on each aspect of the environment. The fundamental issue in the whole process is how to conduct the trade-offs between different components of the environment with different degrees of scheme impact. Clearly, at some stage in the decision-making process, choices will have to be made between scheme options with widely varying effects. For example, Scheme A may have little impact on ecological interests but a very significant impact on archaeological interests whereas Scheme B has little effect on the archaeology or plant life but a considerable impact on wading birds. The procedure does not resolve the conflicts inherent in the making of these choices. What it does do, is to provide a mechanism for systematically reviewing the nature of the choices to be made. This is done in terms of their different degrees of environmental impact without any attempt to quantify the impacts in numerical terms or to value them in monetary terms. In this sense it allows consensus to be reached on the basis of fully informed judgements.

8 Method of summarising ecological change

C. Richards

Introduction

A review of methods used in site assessment indicated that the outcome was often in the form of a large volume of descriptive information. A method that could be used at *any* site for summarising the important points of ecological interest would therefore be preferable. The *habitat and criteria matrix* (Figure 8.1) has been developed to identify the current ecological interest of a site by highlighting aspects of importance as an aid to assessing the significance of any changes. The effects of changes produced by erosion or flooding, or of a coast protection scheme itself, on the ecological interest of the site would be assessed by repeating the matrix to show changes predicted with a range of future scenarios.

The selection of a matrix method over alternatives such as indices is discussed in this chapter. The use of a numerical index or 'score' in each cell of the matrix is of doubtful value and the use of visual indicators was felt to be preferable. There are considerable objections to the use of an overall index of criteria and habitat importance or a single number as a 'final score' which could then be taken as representing the total value of the site. There are also difficulties in the production of a generalisable matrix which can be applied to all coastal sites due to the high degree of variability of coastal habitats.

The matrix as outlined, highlighting features of interest at a site, would be an essential tool in the consultation procedure (Chapter 7) both for the consideration of environmental factors at the initial stages of planning and design and as the basis for trade-offs between different ecological and other components of environmental value.

1. Discussion of matrix – index merits

Matrices
In the habitat and criteria matrix, using a visual indicator rather than a numerical score was preferred for several reasons.

1. A summary of the features of importance should highlight those of particular value, while including other features at the site. In the nature of coastal change, any aspect of site value may be affected.
2. The criteria used should be collectable without the need for an ecological survey, using on-site observation, maps, and brief consultation with nature conservation bodies. Exact figures could be collected later if an ecological survey or EIA was required.
3. The information should not be in such scientific detail as not to be understood by the non-ecologist.
4. A single criterion for site assessment is not feasible. As there may be many reasons for a site's importance, which vary by the characteristics of habitat types, a single criterion cannot adequately reflect a site's value.
5. Basing value on a total score or single figure would result in a loss of information obscuring the features of interest and importance at a site. The effects of erosion or flooding, or of a coast protection scheme, will rarely affect an entire site.
6. The use of numbers in themselves implies objectivity. Evaluation is frequently of a subjective nature as absolute scores cannot be given to every attribute. Where a scale of values is involved, different observers may arrive at different values, making any calculation of a numerical score subjective.
7. If a numerical score is given, there is a danger of mathematical manipulation in a way that is not applicable to ecology. For example, the loss of part of a site may diminish the value of the entire site by more than the value of the portion lost, and also affect the value of adjacent sites, so is not a simple subtraction.
8. Whether particular criteria should be given added weight as being 'more important' would not only involve a subjective judgement, but would also raise mathematical problems, as all scores should be standardised to the same scale even though measured in different units.
9. Multicriteria indices, which total scores for each attribute, run into other mathematical difficulties. By the interactional nature of ecology many criteria overlap, which could be regarded as double counting. To overcome this, criteria should be multiplied. However those criteria which do not overlap should be added together. The

combinations of criteria involved mean that a simple formula is not possible.

Indices
Indices of diversity may be used to give an indication of the diversity of an ecological site. They are most often calculated for species diversity. Although the use of one particular index is not standardised, the two most frequently used are Simpson's diversity index and the Shannon-Weaver (Shannon-Wiener) index.

Simpson's index

$$D = \frac{\displaystyle\sum_{i=1}^{s} n_i(n_i-1)}{n(n-1)} \qquad \text{(Simpson 1949)}$$

Shannon-Weaver index

$$H' = -\sum_{i=1}^{n} p_i.\text{log}p_i \qquad \text{(Shannon and Weaver 1949)}$$

Where s = the number of individuals in a sample or a population
$\quad\quad$ n = the number of individuals in a sample from a population
$\quad\quad$ n_i = the number of individuals in a species i of a sample from a population
$\quad\quad$ p_i = ni/n = the fraction of a sample of individuals belonging to species i

The use of indices is discussed in detail in Washington (1984).
There are a number of disadvantages to their use, and they are not as objective as might appear. Problems arise in the mathematics of the calculations:

1. Simpson's index gives less weight to species which occur in smaller numbers as it is based on multiplications; the Shannon-Weaver is weighted in favour of species which occur in smaller numbers by the use of logarithms.
2. Practical problems can occur during calculation due to lack of

standardisation. For example Simpson's index can be expressed as D, as 1-D, or as 1/D. The logarithm base for Shannon-Weaver has not been standardised and base 10, base 2, and base e have all been used.

3. The scales of indices may be non-linear. This means that a decline, of for example, 4.5 to 4.3 may be more significant than a decline of 1.5 to 1.3.

4. Diversity indices measure 2 components, evenness and variety or numbers of species. Information is required for both. However, as both aspects are being taken into account when the index is being calculated, either factor may be the main influence on the total. For example, the diversity index can increase in value when species numbers decline, if the evenness of their distribution increases.

Problems of comparison arise as the indices are usually calculated for a sample of a population. This should be standardised over the number of sampling points, time, area etc. As this is frequently not the case it should be overcome by standardising the inputs, which would involve using the smallest sampling level, with obvious loss of data.

Biological problems also arise in the use of indices.

1. It may be desirable to exclude certain species from the index depending on the purpose of the calculation, for example 'incidentals', species which just happen to occur at the time of sampling in what would normally be unlikely or adverse conditions, or species planted or introduced by man which would not be desirable as a measure of 'natural' diversity. The treatment of these possible exceptions has not been standardised.

2. If the index is only calculated for flowering plant species diversity, which is most usual, this may not correspond with the value of a site for other species' groups. Certainly vegetation diversity does not necessarily correspond with bird diversity, especially at the coast, where many species may feed on mud-flats of extremely low diversity, dominated by one species. A diversity index alone is not considered appropriate for birds, because of loss of information. The importance of sites may be based on the large size of flocks of one or a few species which congregate for roosting or feeding, frequently on a highly seasonal basis. The normal densities of different bird species vary so information is required on the numbers and distribution of each important or rare species (Fuller and Langslow 1986; Gotmark et al. 1986).

3. The scientific basis for the choice of sites of greatest value would be

undermined if it were based on the use of one species group alone. This is especially true at the coast, where the pioneering species are frequently lichens or Bryophytes, and the value of many sites may be ascribed to Invertebrates. Unfortunately it would not be possible to use diversity indices for all species at a site, partly due to lack of knowledge of the distribution and occurrence of many species groups and also to the time required for site surveys, which would be prohibitive. This suggests that habitat criteria, which could indicate sufficient diversity to cover the requirements of as many taxa as possible, would be of greater validity in the assessment of value of sites.

4. Diversity in unstable and developing habitats is likely to be low, but not necessarily of lower value than a habitat of high diversity. A diversity index for a site could then be high or low without this giving any indication of its comparative or even absolute value. It would be more usual to use the index to compare habitats of the same type, so as to compare like with like.

Several authors, including Usher (1986), agree that species richness is a better measure of diversity than a diversity index. Washington (1984) comes to the conclusion that the continued use of Shannon-Weaver is due to its 'entrenched nature' rather than to any biological relevance.

In the Hengistbury report, the Shannon-Weaver diversity index was used for habitats. Biologically, as well as the previously mentioned mathematical limitations, there are many problems with this particular application. Only one aspect of the value of habitats is being addressed: that of diversity based on numbers and evenness. At any one site, it is not necessarily desirable or even likely that the habitats present will be distributed with any kind of spatial evenness, if several are present at all. One of the main aspects of value of mud-flats and salt-marshes is their large extent, but the rarity of coastal lagoons means that a small area – down to .5 ha. for SSSI assessment – is still of high value.

The diversity of habitats was one of the main points of interest at Christchurch Harbour. Only this one aspect of the ecological value was measured, and it is one which need not necessarily occur at another site. Other aspects of value cannot be measured directly by such an index.

Another feature at the site was the transition from freshwater to saltwater marsh. Where these gradual changes occur, for example where vegetation succession has proceeded uninterrupted over time, the definition and delineation of each habitat type becomes subjective.

Consequently any diversity index is no longer comparable. The broad categories of habitat type used by Ratcliffe (1977) may also include considerable within-habitat diversity, with greater variations possible within some habitats than others. Again comparisons can only be made between similar habitats. Although a more exact division of habitat types would be possible, for example based on the National Vegetation Classification based on vegetation communities, this would have the disadvantages of being less easily understood by the non-specialist and also of increasing the number of site divisions, with greater difficulty of comparative assessment.

There may not necessarily be any rare species at a site, but where they occur they are generally of considerable interest to the public and may be subject to protective legislation under the Wildlife and Countryside Act. Rare habitat types, perhaps due to specialised physico-chemical conditions, or habitats declining due to man's activities, should also be regarded as of especial value, and some may receive legal protection under the EEC Habitats Directive. Diversity indices do not consider any weighted values.

2. The proposed methodology

Most methods of evaluating ecological sites are for the selection of sites for nature conservation purposes, either for designation or to assess the type of management required. These sources have been drawn on in the development of the criteria for the matrix, in particular Ratcliffe (1977) and Ranwell (Ratcliffe 1986), and the most useful criteria extracted or adapted to our requirements.

The matrix is not intended to be a quick method of site assessment, but rather a summary of ecological information available. This information may already have been gathered for designation or management purposes, or an ecological survey may be required.

At coastal sites threatened by erosion or flooding, several factors have to be taken into consideration. The planners and engineers involved at a site need to know the factors of ecological value; which of these factors will be affected by erosion or flooding; and whether a coast protection scheme will protect features of value or be ecologically damaging in itself, in which case an alternative scheme or scheme modification may be possible without such adverse impacts.

There is a need for comprehensive information to be presented in a systematic and comprehensible way for non-ecological specialists. The suggested approach is to summarise the key information on a series of matrices to show:

1. the situation as it is now;
2. the probable effects in the future with continued erosion or flooding;
3. the with-scheme effects.

The matrix that has been developed is intended to be a broad summary of features of ecological value at a site. Language has been kept as simple as possible to be comprehensive to non-ecologists, hence words such as 'taxa' or 'para-maritime' normally used by ecologists have been avoided. Additional notes and explanations may be required to elaborate those features of value which are highlighted by a study – for example, whether a physico-chemical specialisation is hydrological or geological, and where change occurs, why.

Information on whether a site is designated (or not) has not been included on the matrix because this is information which would be obtained in the normal course of site investigation. Moreover, as non-designation does not mean a site is without ecological value, this factor should not be used as a criterion of itself. If a site is already designated, then the information on its ecological interest should be readily obtainable. If it is not designated, then it is likely that local naturalists groups may still know about or be involved in keeping records at a site. There are a number of such voluntary and other organisations which may be involved at ecological sites. English Nature and the local authority would usually know about these but this is not always the case – a list of bodies which should be contacted will be drawn up for the manual.

The matrix has been designed to be used with the different habitats which may be present at a site. Nine criteria have been selected, and visual indicators are used in the cells where they are applicable. Visual indicators have been used instead of numbers for the reasons given earlier.

The criteria use a three-point scale: for example large, medium and small; or International/National, Regional and Local. Subjective opinions will still arise in any assessment, but it was felt that the standing of many species and habitats can be recognised at the above levels and that a large number of categories would introduce spurious precision. In addition, knowing the relative scale of importance can be of practical value to engineers and planners for assessing site value, and also for assessing the implications of possible action. Although features of local value at an undesignated site would be recognised by ecologists as of less 'importance', there may well still be a high level of interest and concern for a particular site and the effects of any changes on them should still be taken into account in a systematic way.

Habitat categories
Marine habitats may appear to be affected by a comparatively limited number of schemes, for example those involving dredging, or offshore constructions. But these are only direct effects. Indirect effects by changed patterns of sediment supply could also affect a marine site, so consultation with the Marine Conservation Society is always desirable.

Lagoons may occupy an ambiguous position. Whether some lagoons should be considered as a marine habitat is dependent on which authorities are used, as Barnes' (1989) list of 41 lagoons does not agree with other interpretations of what is meant by a lagoon (e.g. Gubbay 1988). They have been placed in the category of maritime habitats with a note that other inter-tidal water bodies should be included in the marine category.

The maritime habitats listed in the matrix follow those of Ratcliffe (1977) in the Nature Conservation Review as being the simplest and most generally known and accepted. Although there may be boundary or descriptive problems with categories of habitat, a more complex system would be unacceptable in terms of the uses to which the matrix will be put – that is, being interpreted by engineers and planners.

Terrestrial habitats are listed in four categories, although it is recognised that there may be variants within the categories and gradients between them.

Criteria
Habitat size. Using the absolute size of each habitat can only be appropriate where comparisons are being made within single habitat types. Otherwise it is likely that habitats which are by their nature small could be regarded as less important even though they may be one of the largest of their habitat type. The size grades developed by Ranwell (Ratcliffe 1986) have been contracted to fit the matrix scale, but these are only suggested for maritime habitats – size categories for lagoons have not been suggested and can be discussed later. Habitat diversity is not included as a separate criterion, but where several habitats and sub-habitats are present this will be indicated by the larger numbers of visual indicators present in the top row of the matrix.

Sub-habitats. The number of sub-habitats included has been reduced to a minimum for simplicity – the system used for Sites of Special Scientific Interest (SSSI) assessment based on the National Vegetation Classification (Nature Conservancy Council 1989) was considered to have too many subdivisions for non-ecologists to understand, but could be used for a full-scale ecological survey. In some instances the examples of succession provided by within-habitat changes can be one of the main points of interest at a coastal site. However, for others, such as mudflats, its homogeneity may be one of its main characteristics. It must always therefore be stressed that sub-habitats are only of value where they might be expected to be present, and a habitat without different sub-habitats is not necessarily of lesser value. Whether the size of sub-habitats can be assessed in the same way as that of the entire habitat, that is by relative size, or whether proportions should be used, or an indication of presence or absence, is open to discussion.

The *combinatory value* of a site, that is, its ecological and spatial relationship to other sites of interest, is of particular importance at the coast where fragmentation of sites due to development is a perennial problem. It should be pointed out here, however, that sites isolated by urban and other development may be of great value locally, and that consequently such a site could give rise to strong feelings apparently out of proportion to its ecological value.

Physico-chemical specialisation may be due to several factors, and these should be itemised and summarised where present, in the text or as footnotes. This aspect of a site's value may be especially liable to change at the coast – for example, the hydrological regime from more specialised brackish to salt as a result of seawater flooding, or to freshwater after the construction of impermeable coast protection works.

Naturalness is a measure of the level of disturbance at a site. Lack of disturbance directly by *people* rather than by past human activities, has been stressed so that unimproved grazed marshes could be included in the top category. A site degraded, for example, by overgrazing or overtrampling by animals would obviously be in the lower category. The word 'structures' was used in the definition of visual indicators, rather than buildings, so that, for example, telephone or electricity pylons, which would require regular access for maintenance, would be included.

This criterion has not been used in the same sense as in the Nature Conservation Review (Ratcliffe 1977) as unmodified vegetation not altered by man's activities. The less restrictive definition has been adopted for several reasons. First, this criterion would be rated differently according to the area concerned. Second, it may also be difficult to assess the degree of past human intervention. Finally, patterns of grazing, drainage modifications, or even old borrow pits for coast protection works, can increase diversity of habitat and species and produce habitats of interest and value.

Rare species may have legal implications under the Wildlife and Countryside Act. It is also one of the main questions asked by the general public about a wildlife site. The species concerned should be itemised separately in the text accompanying the matrix.

Important *populations of interest* have been grouped together. Birds have been separated from other vertebrates because of the high level of information available. Non-flowering plants have been separated from flowering and may include marine algae and also pioneering lichens and Bryophytes as these may become crowded out and disappear where a site is stabilised by coast protection works.

A complete list of taxonomic groups is not essential as it obscures the important issues – a more comprehensive list would be drawn up for an ecological survey.

Specialist research interest was certainly held by Ratcliffe (1977) to enhance the ecological value of a site. As one of the major features of coastal sites is change, then knowledge of the changes and processes of change over time can only increase a site's value. The destruction or damage of a studied site could therefore be considered to cause a greater loss than a similar loss at an unresearched site.

Here we are recommending that educational use of a site, for example by school and college students, should not be considered in the same category as research. Educational uses could be better described as recreation – and educational use, by trampling and collecting of specimens, may well be detrimental to a site's ecology.

Rare and declining habitats are an important factor when considering the value of habitats. Some rare habitats may be protected in the near future under the EEC Habitats Directive. *Guidelines for Selection of Biological SSSIs* (NCC 1989) gives some parameters for rare habitats at a national level, and considers that any habitat with a total area under 10,000 ha. can be regarded as rare. These could be listed in the manual, but it may not be desirable to do so in view of possible future changes. They would include at present coastal heath over 10 ha., although even smaller fragments may be of national value if they also have high physico-chemical specialisation; lagoons over .5 ha.; larger shingle features over 25 ha.; with unimproved grazing marsh as among the most rapidly declining.

Some Nature Conservation Review criteria which have not been included in the matrix are:

Fragility – in terms of re-creatability, habitats which are least re-creatable are also likely to be those which are rarest. In terms of vulnerability, this is the threat posed by the erosion or flooding for which the coastal protection scheme is being considered.

Typicalness – this is a difficult criterion to apply as it is usually the special features of interest at a site that are being considered.

Where there are several criteria of lower value, no rare species and high naturalness, this may be considered a 'typical' site.

Potential value – that is, could the site or will the site improve or be improved with time? This is again a difficult criterion to apply, as it is more suitable for nature conservation management requirements than in terms of coastal protection.

Intrinsic appeal – this is a social rather than an ecological judgement.

To come to the last column and the last row in the matrix, *Overall Importance of Criteria*, and *Overall Importance of Habitat*. Having argued against a numerical score which can be totalled, resulting in a loss of information, it may seem inappropriate to include these summaries in the matrix for similar reasons. Unlike a numerical score, however, the visual indicators are perhaps less easily used separately away from the matrix itself, and consequently for the time being they are being included and the reaction to their use assessed.

The summation of indicators would be unsuitable for either category – for example, for criteria, although it is possible that several small habitats could equal a medium-sized site, most criteria cannot be totalled: three trampled or polluted habitats could never become an unpolluted site. For habitats, the sum of a naturally more diverse and mature habitat would generally be higher than the pioneer, such as a mudflat.

There are two possible alternatives: either the highest visual indicator in a row or column could be used to show the overall importance, or an assessment of the average of the indicators present, which would be more subjective as fractions would not be possible. Using the highest indicator present would give a more consistent approach, but is not very flexible. Choosing a more subjective method does raise the issue of whether some criteria might be regarded as more important than others.

The final cell, which could receive the label 'overall importance of site', is one that I feel should be excluded from the matrix. However, whether a site is of major or national/ international importance, of regional importance, or of local importance, is probably a judgement which can be made about a site, so long as it is accepted that it is simply a *general* indication of the level of value. Since the purpose of the matrices is not to enable the comparable ranking of different sites, but to summarise the changes which would result either from a coast protection scheme or doing nothing, the summary conclusion that is required is that as to the relative desirability of the different options. That summary conclusion is a relative judgement and dependent upon what are the feasible options.

Habitats / Criteria	Marine[1] Mudflats	Maritime[2] Saltmarsh	Maritime[2] Vegetated shingle	Maritime[2] Dunes	Lagoons	Cliffs	Terrestrial[2] Fresh water	Grass land	Heath	Wood land	Overall importance of criteria
Size of habitat[3]											
Size of sub-habitats[4]		L H B G	P H	M F S							
Combinatory value[5]											
Physico-chemical specialisation[6]											
Naturalness[7]											
Rare species[8]											
Populations of interest[9] Birds											
Other vertebrates											
Invertebrates											
Flora: flowering											
non - flowering											
Specialist research interest[10]											
Rare/declining habitats[11]											
Overall importance of habitat											

L=Low   P=Pioneer   M=Mobile
H=High   H=Shingle   F=Fixed

Figure 8.1 Habitat-criteria matrix

Key to habitat – criteria matrix

[1] Marine: The marine habitat may be defined as below low water mark and other inter-tidal habitats not included in categories of maritime habitats. Classification of marine habitats is more complex than can be represented on the matrix. For details consult: *A Coastal Directory for Marine Conservation* (Gubbay, 1988) and/or the Marine Conservations Society.

[2] Maritime and Terrestrial: Habitat divisions based on Ratcliffe (1977). Consult English Nature, Local Authority ecologist and any management body for the site. These organisations should have information on any other bodies which may be involved at the site.

[3] Size of habitats: Habitat size category does not depend on actual extent at the site but is assessed relative to the size range of that habitat in general. Guidance on this for maritime and terrestrial habitats is given in Ranwell's semi-quantitative index (Ratcliffe, 1986). Other habitats are more complex, e.g. lagoons have several alternative categorisations. (Gubbay, 1988; Barnes, 1989).

[4] Size of sub-habitats: Where applicable, habitats may be separated into sub-habitats, if the information is available. NB: Habitats which by their nature have no sub-habitats are not necessarily of less value.

[5] Combinatory value: Applicable where site is adjacent to other similar habitats, either immediately adjacent or as part of a sequence with interbreeding populations or migratory species movements.

[6] Physico-chemical specialisation: indicates rare or unusual conditions of geology, soils, sediment, hydrology or geomorphology.

[7] Naturalness: Based on a visual, on-site, assessment of relative degree of disturbance.

[8] Rare species: Determined according to criteria for rare species at International, National, Regional and Local scale.

[9] Important populations of interest: Determined according to International, National, Regional and Local importance. NB: Information may not be available for all species groups.

[10] Specialist research interest: Related to amount of recorded history of past research and amount of on-going research.

[11] Rare/Declining habitats: Determined according to extent of decline; whether International, National, Regional or Local.

The application of the matrix to the three situations: current site conditions, a site with continued erosion and/or flooding, and a site with a proposed coast protection scheme, is better discussed with reference to a case study rather than in principle. The next chapter discusses the application of the matrix approach to the ecological component in a case study of Hengistbury Head.

References

Barnes, R. S. K. (1989) The Coastal Lagoons of Britain: an Overview and Conservation Appraisal, *Biological Conservation* 49: 295–313.

Fuller, R. J. and Langslow, D. R. (1986) Ornithological Evaluation for Wildlife Conservation in Usher, M. B. (ed.) *Wildlife Conservation Evaluation*, London: Chapman and Hall. pp. 247–69.

Gotmark, F., Ahlund, M. and Eriksson, M. O. G. (1986) Are indices reliable for assessing the conservation value of natural areas? An avian case study, *Biological Conservation* 38: 55–73.

Gubbay, S. (ed.) (1988) *A Coastal Directory for Marine Nature Conservation*, Ross-on-Wye: Marine Conservation Society.

Nature Conservancy Council (1989) *Guidelines for the selection of biological SSSIs*, Peterborough: NCC.

Parker, D. J. and Thompson, P. M. (1988) An 'Extended' Economic Appraisal of Coast Protection Works: a Case Study of Hengistbury Head, England, *Ocean and Shoreline Management* 11: 45–72.

Ratcliffe, D. A. (ed.) (1977) *A Nature Conservation Review, Vol. 1*, Cambridge: Cambridge University Press.

Ratcliffe, D. A. (1986) Selection of important areas for wildlife conservation in Great Britain: the Nature Conservancy Council's approach, in Usher, M. B. (ed.) *Wildlife Conservation Evaluation*, London: Chapman & Hall, 135–59.

Simpson, E. H. (1949) Measurement of Diversity, *Nature* 163 (4148): 688.

Shannon, C. E. and Weaver, W. (1949) *The Mathematical Theory of Communication*, Urbana: University of Illinois Press.

Thompson, P. M., Parker, D. J., Coker, A., Grant, E., Penning-Rowsell, E. and Suleman, M. (1987) *The Economic and Environmental Impacts of Coast Erosion and Protection: A Case Study of Hengistbury Head and Christchurch Harbour, England*, Enfield: Middlesex Polytechnic Geography and Planning Paper No. 19.

Usher, M. B. (ed.) (1986) *Wildlife Conservation Evaluation*, London: Chapman & Hall, 247–69.

Washington, H. G. (1984) Diversity, Biotic and Similarity Indices, *Water Research* 18,6: 653–94.

9 A case study of Hengistbury Head

A. Coker

Introduction

A scheme which the Flood Hazard Research Centre has already assessed using an 'extended' benefit-cost analysis is at Hengistbury Head and Christchurch Harbour, Dorset (Parker and Thompson 1988). This example differs from the situation at many coastal sites in that the major environmental damage would not be caused by the scheme itself but would occur from losses resultant upon flooding in the absence of a coastal protection scheme (Figure 9.1).

Although the extended appraisal incorporated ecological, archaeo-logical, geological and recreational impacts of erosion and flooding at the site, only the recreational element was valued in economic terms. An attempt to quantify the gains and losses for the other elements was mainly in descriptive terms which included an indication of the area of the site to be affected. The only quantification was of the ecological component, using the Shannon-Weaver index of habitat diversity to give an idea of the variation in diversity of habitat types with flooding or erosion.It is the diversity of habitat types which is one of the main reasons why the area has been designated as a Site of Special Scientific Interest (SSSI).

In this particular case, the economic benefits of a coast protection scheme were adequate, when assessed in terms of conventional economic benefits, including recreational benefits, to offset the engineering costs of the scheme. In hindsight, it is interesting to see whether a more fully quantified assessment of environmental changes can be derived and, if so, how such an evaluation of the ecological component of site interest could be carried out in practice.

The approach adopted in the 1986 study was to divide the area into ecological divisions according to habitat type and to summarise the ecological information for each division in a descriptive manner (Parker and Thompson 1988; Thompson et al. 1987).

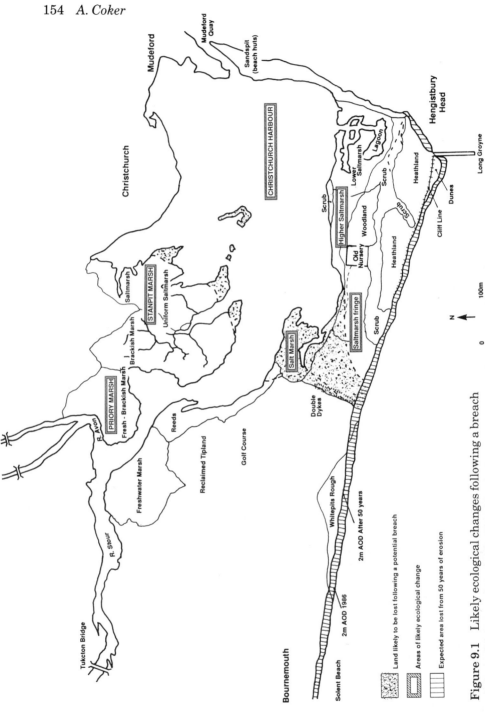

Figure 9.1   Likely ecological changes following a breach

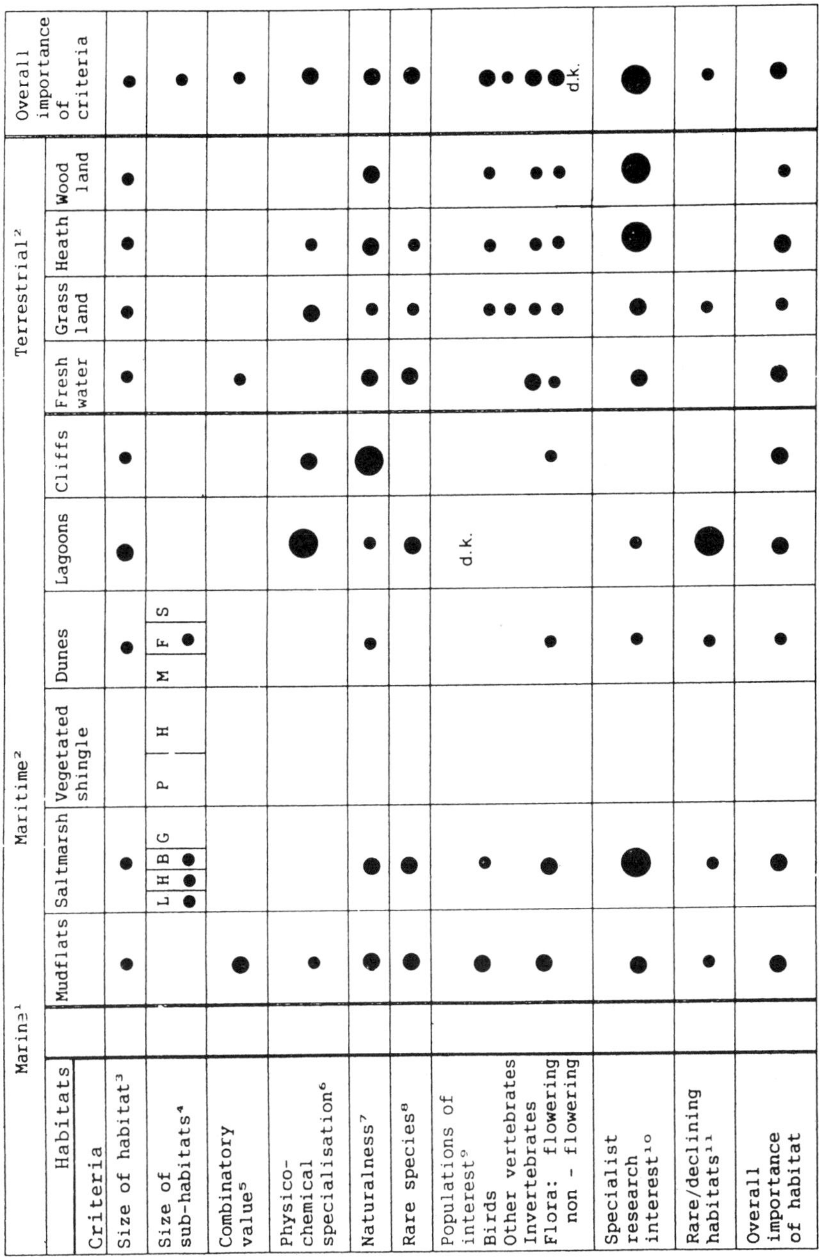

Figure 9.2i Application of matrix method to Hengistbury–Christchurch: Matrix 1: Current situation (pre-scheme)

Legend:

L=Low
H=High
B=Brackish
G=Grazed

P=Pioneer
H=Shingle heath

M=Mobile
F=Fixed
S=Slacks

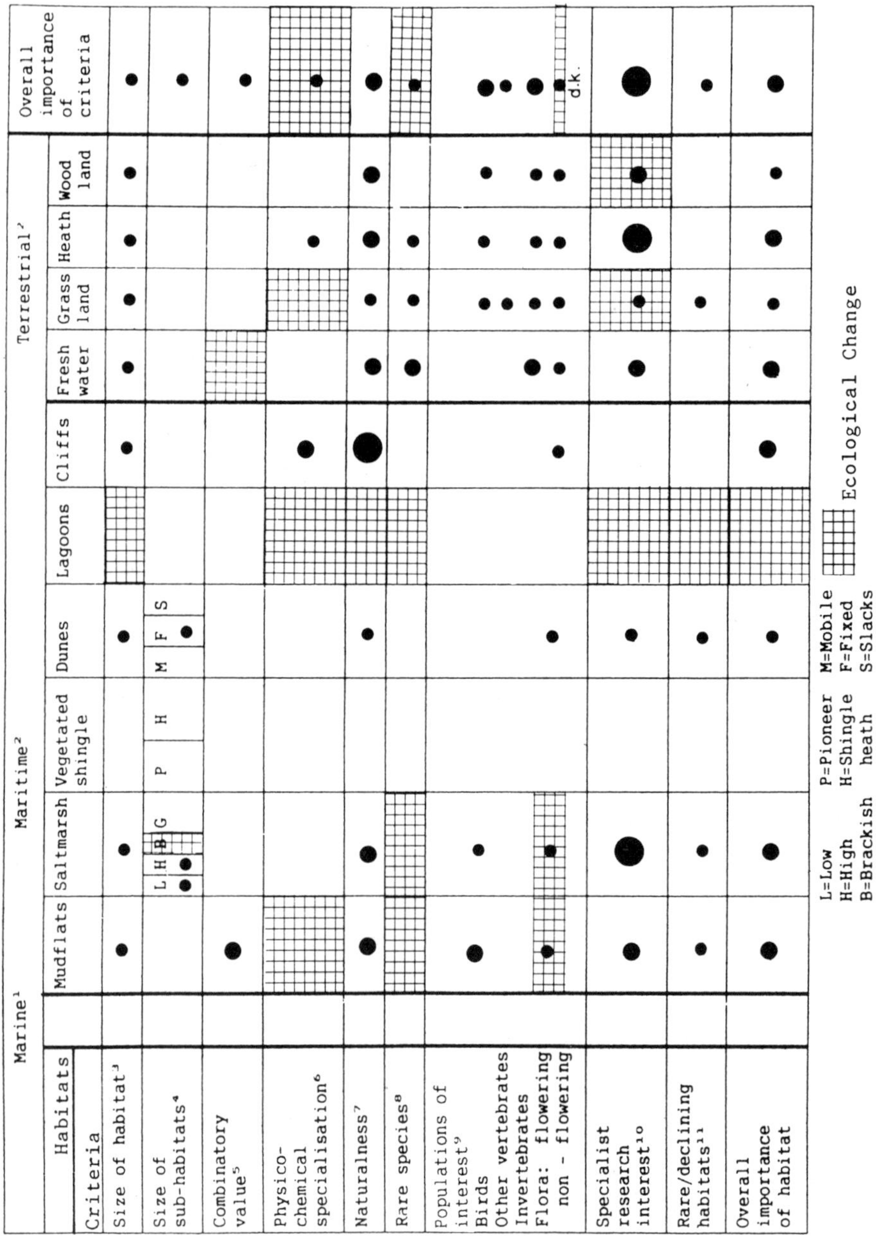
Marine[1]
Maritime[2]
Terrestrial[2]
Habitats
Criteria
Mudflats
Saltmarsh
Vegetated shingle
Dunes
Lagoons
Cliffs
Fresh water
Grass land
Heath
Wood land
Overall importance of criteria
Size of habitat[3]
Size of sub-habitats[4]
L H B G
P H
M F S
Combinatory value[5]
Physico-chemical specialisation[6]
Naturalness[7]
Rare species[8]
Populations of interest[9]
Birds
Other vertebrates
Invertebrates
Flora: flowering
non - flowering
d.k.
Specialist research interest[10]
Rare/declining habitats[11]
Overall importance of habitat
L=Low
H=High
B=Brackish
G=Grazed
P=Pioneer
H=Shingle heath
M=Mobile
F=Fixed
S=Slacks
Ecological Change

Figure 9.2ii Matrix 2: Future situation without coast protection (assumes a breach and erosion)

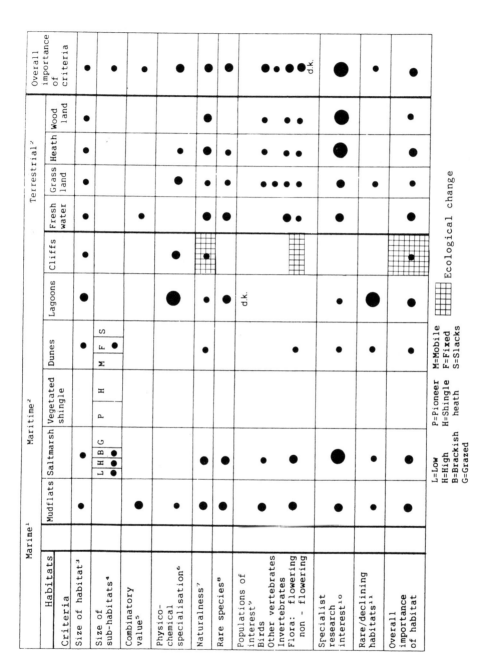

Figure 9.2iii Matrix 3: Future situation with coast protection

Key to the habitat – criteria matrix

[1] Marine: The marine habitat may be defined as below low water mark and other inter-tidal habitats not included in categories of maritime habitats. Classification of marine habitats is more complex than can be represented on the matrix. For details consult: *A Coastal Directory for Marine Conservation* (Gubbay, 1988) and/or the Marine Conservations Society.

[2] Maritime and Terrestrial: Habitat divisions based on Ratcliffe (1977). Consult English Nature, Local Authority ecologist and any management body for the site. These organisations should have information on any other bodies which may be involved at the site.

[3] Size of habitats:

- ● large
- ● medium
- • small

Habitat size category does not depend on actual extent at the site but is assessed relative to the size range of that habitat in general.

Examples:

Mudflats		*Saltmarsh and sand dunes*
Area (ha)		Area (ha)
≤ 1600	●	≤ 400
400–1599	●	80–399
≥ 400	•	≥ 80

Vegetated shingle		*Cliffs*
Area (ha)		Undisturbed run of cliff length (km)
≤ 80	●	≤ 40
20–79	●	8–39
≥ 20	•	≥ 8

(Based on Ranwell's semi-quantitative index (Ratcliffe 1986))

Other habitats are more complex, e.g. lagoons have several alternative categorisations (Gubbay 1988; Barnes 1989).

[4] Size of sub-habitats: Where applicable, habitats may be separated in sub-habitats, if the information is available.

- ● large
- ● medium   criteria to be determined
- • small

NB: Habitats which by their nature have no sub-habitats are not necessarily of less value.

[5] Combinatory value: i.e. whether adjacent to other similar habitat sites, either immediately adjacent or as part of a sequence with interbreeding populations or migratory species movements.

- Adjacent to another habitat site of International/ National value
- Adjacent to another habitat site of Regional value
- Adjacent to another habitat site of Local value

[6] Physico-chemical specialisation: rare or unusual conditions of geology, soils, sediment, hydrology, or geomorphology.

- Internationally-nationally rare
- Regionally rare
- Locally rare

[7] Naturalness: a visual assessment on-site.

- Undisturbed by people
- Some pathways, some litter
- Structures, tracks, trampling, polluted water

[8] Rare species:

- Wildlife and Countryside Act protected species, International and British Red Data Book species
- Regionally rare species, nationally rare species not included in the above
- Locally rare species

[9] Important populations of interest:

- Internationally/nationally important populations
- Regionally-Locally important populations
- Representative interest

NB: Information may not be available for all the species groups

[10] Specialist research interest:

- Recorded history of past research and on-going research
- Recorded history or future research plans
- Some records

---

[11] Rare/declining habitats:

- ● Internationally/Nationally rare/declining (defined in general)
- ● Regionally rare/declining (defined by region)
- • Locally rare/declining (defined by site)

This paper presents a re-evaluation of the ecological element of the study, in the form of matrices which show the relative importance of each of the components of ecological value in a systematic visual form in which it can be more easily comprehended by the non-ecologist.

A set of three matrices has been produced summarising the relative ecological value of the site in the current situation (Figure 9.2i), without a coastal protection scheme (Figure 9.2ii), and with one (Figure 9.2iii). If we accept the uncertainties associated with the prediction of ecological change, then comparison of these matrices enables a relative evaluation to be made of the changes in ecological interest under different conditions.

In Chapter 8 the justification for using visual indicators rather than a numerical scoring system in the matrices was outlined. This case study illustrates the application of the matrix to the ecological information for Hengistbury Head.

Ecological interest of the site under existing conditions

It can be seen from Figure 9.2i that the ecological interest of the location results from its high diversity of habitats within a small area rather than from outstanding ecological importance of any individual habitat or species. All habitats except shingle are represented in the area. In the original study, 15 ecological divisions (units) were identified, each being a discrete area supporting specific habitats, e.g. the areas of Higher & Lower Saltmarsh north of the headland. In creating these categories the ecological importance of the harbour itself was not considered. Subsequently, the classification of coastal lagoon habitats has been clarified (Barnes 1989) and a reappraisal indicated that the harbour could have been considered as a lagoon within Barnes' classification, thus making a 16th unit.

There are two important stages in completing the matrices:

1 Allocating values to cells

The matrix shows clearly that the value of the site comprises four main components:

The first is its high diversity of habitat types. Every coastal habitat except shingle is represented, and the sub-habitats of saltmarsh include low, high and brackish marsh although areas of each are small in size in comparison with the national size range of these habitats.

Second, the physico-chemical characteristics of the lagoon area and its national rarity as a habitat contribute to the overall site value.

The third important factor is the naturalness of the cliffs on the headland.

Fourth, the research information available for the saltmarsh and wind-trimmed heath in terms of their vegetation and for the woodland in relation to its ornithological records make a significant contribution to the value of the site.

The combinatory role of the mudflats, i.e. their ecological role in a wider context than that of this site alone, is given an intermediate sized indicator because of the inter-relationship with other sites of regional value for example, as a feeding ground for bird species using other sites such as Poole Harbour.

It can be seen that use of visual indicators in the matrix gives a straightforward visual way of presenting information about the site overall which can be easily assimilated.

2 Combining values to give assessment of overall importance

The way in which these values are combined to show the overall importance of each criterion (rows) and each habitat (columns) must be on the basis of estimates by specialists completing the matrix.

Arriving at the values in the final columns is *not* comparable either with summing each component value, as with a numerical scale, or taking the arithmetic mean; neither does it take the maximum value in the row or column as the maximum overall.

The way in which we have handled this is to make a judgement – which does reflect a type of averaging process but is not as mechanistic as taking a mean. This raises the fundamental issue of the reliability of the approach. For example, where we have made the judgement that, because of the large amount of recorded information in three of the habitats, this criterion should be given the highest category of importance overall, other ecologists might have arrived at a different judgement about the assessment of overall importance of research interest in this case.

It is important to stress that the function of the matrix is for comparative purposes only, to enable the significant changes which would occur both with and without a coastal protection scheme to be clearly identified in order to make a judgement about the vulnerability of the area overall to changes. Clearly, if there are differences in professional judgement about the overall importance of specific criteria which will be affected by a scheme, then it could be better not to attempt any overall summation.

Changes in ecological interest of site without coastal protection scheme

The main changes which could occur if the coast were to be breached at the lowest point, Double Dykes, were predicted by coastal ecologists and are as shown in Figure 9.1.

The main changes anticipated are:

1. Christchurch Harbour, which is at present enclosed by the headland and neck of land and only open to the sea at the narrow sheltered harbour entrance to the east, would be open to the sea and its physico-chemical characteristics altered.
2. Some habitats would be lost altogether through increased erosion, for example the 15 hectares of unimproved grassland at Double Dykes, some of the lower marsh at Stanpit, and the dry grassland at Crouch Hill.
3. Other habitats would experience altered conditions, specifically a change from brackish to saline conditions and greater flooding of the main marshland areas overall, which would be likely to lead to a loss in the gradation between both brackish and salt-marsh and between lower and upper marsh at Stanpit.

So, if each area of different habitat is considered as an ecological unit, overall there would be a reduction from 15 to 11 units with a breach.

This has been represented in Matrix 2 (Fig 9.2ii) as follows:

1. Loss of the lagoon features.
2. Loss of the sub-habitat of brackish marsh.
3. Loss in rare species of mudflats and saltmarsh e.g. *Eleocharis parvula*.

In this example, all the changes can be considered as representing an ecological loss although it is recognised that there could be some gains which were not identified.

Changes in ecological interest of site with coastal protection scheme

At Hengistbury Head the changes caused by the proposed coastal protection scheme are restricted in scope but would result in losses to the cliff area and would clearly be an ecological cost of the scheme in the sense that the geological site interest would be reduced (Fig.9.2iii).

Conclusion

As already pointed out, in this case study the main ecological losses would result from flooding following a breach without a coastal protection scheme. Hence the ecological losses which would occur without a scheme become one of the benefits of the scheme. However, at many coastal sites, due to the dynamic nature of coastal habitats, their ecological interest may be affected more by the development of a coastal protection scheme than due to natural changes without one – in such cases the ecological changes to the site would have to be counted as one of the costs of the scheme.

This study did not attempt to predict the beneficial aspects of a breach, in ecological terms. This reflects the underlying premise on which all coast protection engineering is based; that, as flooding results in losses, coast protection must be beneficial. However, this assumption does not always apply in the case of ecological interests. As pointed out in the discussion of the Aldeburgh case study (Chapter 5), there could be significant ecological gains if Christchurch Harbour were to become an open estuary. However, there is always more uncertainty attached to the prediction of possible ecological gains compared with the obvious losses which would be sustained by a breach at Hengistbury. Allowing natural changes to take place may create an improvement, ecologically-speaking, but these are unlikely to be allowed to take place unless their ecological value can be clearly demonstrated as greater than other losses which would be sustained without any coastal protection. Therefore a full appraisal should attempt to predict the significance of the anticipated gains in ecological terms as well as the inevitable losses.

The use of the ecological matrices enables the beneficial and detrimental changes both with and without a scheme to be clearly identified and the next stage in the process then becomes one of how to balance out one against the other.

Only the ecological interests of the site have been presented here using the matrix, although the area also contains considerable archaeological interest as outlined by Thompson et al. (1987). In this case, the ecological and archaeological interests tend to coincide. A breach at Double Dykes would result in the loss of a significant part of the Iron Age site as well as loss of the old grassland which covers it. At other sites the situation might not be so straighforward, with different scheme options having differential degrees of impact on the various components of the site. At this site, for example, we can see how ecological and geological interests do not coincide, and how it may not be possible to reach a compromise between these two interests.

If we consider all these interests to be beyond comparative valuation, we fail to contribute to the decision-making processes which have to take place in a systematic way. The development of methods which can be easily comprehended by the non-specialist should facilitate decision-making. A first stage in this process is to bring the diverse aspects of ecological value into an acceptable common framework of measures, such as the matrices used here. With rising relative sea levels decisions about priorities and trade-offs could become increasingly important.

References

Barnes, R. S. K. (1989) The coastal lagoons of Britain: an overview and conservation appraisal, *Biological Conservation* 49:295–313.

Parker, D. J. and Thompson, P. M. (1988) An 'extended' economic appraisal of coast protection works: a case study of Hengistbury Head, England, *Ocean and Shoreline Management* 11:45–72.

Thompson, P. M., Parker, D. J., Coker, A., Grant, E., Penning-Rowsell, E. and Suleman, M. (1987) *The economic and environmental impacts of coast erosion and protection: a case study of Hengistbury Head and Christchurch Harbour, England*, Enfield: Middlesex Polytechnic Geography and Planning Paper No. 19.

9 Commentary

Although the matrix approach appears to offer a useful way in which to summarise information about ecological and other environmental factors, there are some reservations associated with its use. As natural systems are usually complex, any attempt to present information about them in a simplified form will be interpreted by some as a distortion. It is evident that a matrix cannot show all the interconnections in a complex ecosystem but it needs to be seen in the context for which it has been designed. That is to enable comparisons between the effects of different courses of action rather than as an attempt to display all the details of a complex system. Given this function, it becomes clear that the purpose of the matrix is to identify and highlight only those factors of ecological importance which will be affected by different scenarios of action or inaction.

One of the main problems with the completion of a matrix is that, because making even a relative evaluation is difficult, there is a natural reticence over attempts to summarise the importance of various ecological components in the cells of a matrix. In particular, any attempt to quantify the importance, whether in numerical terms or by the use of visual indicators, is seen by some as misleading. Even if visual indicators are used instead of numbers in the cells of the matrix, there is inevitably an element of subjective professional judgement required to decide upon their size. Ecologists are used to making evaluations on the basis of accumulated knowledge which may be difficult, or misleading, to express as absolute values.

A further problem with site evaluation is that sometimes the available information is open to interpretation in a number of ways which may even be contradictory, depending on the particular perspective of the professional ecologist. An example of this in the case of Hengistbury Head is that Christchurch Harbour has been categorised by one ecologist as a lagoon due to its physical features whereas a more general interpretation of its biological characteristics is that they are estuarine.

The handling of the 'do nothing' option has already been referred to in previous chapters and this can also be seen as one of the most problematic aspects of the use of the matrices in this case study. In Christchurch Harbour more interesting habitats might be formed by a breach, in the opinion of some ecologists. This illustrates the fact that it is comparatively straightforward for the destructive aspects of the future situation to be identified, but the creation of new habitats which could be as valuable, or more so, is far more difficult to predict. This is especially relevant in view of scenarios of future sea level rise in which coast protection options might have to include the abandonment of land and the reversion to earlier sea defences (Clayton 1991). Thus land which is at present agricultural could revert to salt marsh, and would be seen by some as a considerable ecological gain although in agricultural terms and in the 'popular perception' it would be regarded as a loss. However, it is always easier to identify changes which would make later conditions suitable for a particular species than it is to predict the precise ecological conditions which would develop.

This raises the question of how to treat missing information when completing the matrices. The use of a question mark appears to be a valid way of indicating missing ecological data. The information could then be obtained from further ecological survey or research if a fuller assessment were required. However, other 'unknowns' may arise, such as unknown time-scales or unknown degrees of change. The most acceptable way to present these uncertainties is clearly to indicate them in notes to accompany the matrix rather than to try and increase the complexity of the matrix in order to encompass them.

It is suggested that the matrix could also be used as a checklist for an EIA although it should be recognised that the function of the matrix in the context outlined here is to summarise ecological value at a site for non-specialists. Although the same information could be useful in an EIA it is important to note that these matrices will be applied even to sites where an EIA is not merited. The matrix can also be used in the initial stages of a study to indicate whether the changes are likely to be significant. Hence it could contribute to the decision of whether the proposed scheme is sufficiently significant to require an EIA.

Due to the specific characteristics of many coastal sites, it is difficult to design a matrix which can adequately take these into account at the same time as being generally applicable. It is not surprising that some ecologists consider the matrices do not cover certain aspects in sufficient detail. Marine habitats in particular have only recently been fully classified (Gubbay 1990) and could perhaps be seen to justify a separate matrix to do justice to their complexity. Many of the criteria cannot be applied to a marine habitat in the same way as to maritime or terrestrial habitats. For example, additional criteria would be required to show position in the biogeographic region. A marine matrix would have to take into account at least four other dimensions: substrate, wave exposure, tidal streams and other modifiers, and community characteristics. In the marine habitat, communities are a more important basis than individual species for designating sites as important. However, if the matrices become too complex then they lose their value of presenting the significant factors for non-specialists.

The issue of whether or not to prioritise sites in order of ecological importance is bound to arise. However, it is not the function of the matrices to prioritise sites according to their ecological interest per se. The need for prioritisation only arises in the case of individual sites where comparisons are being made between the relative ecological impact of different courses of action, such as different scheme options, and here, it is the importance of the impact which needs to be prioritised. However, on a larger scale of coastal planning, where a range of strategies may be available each of which could have an impact on different sites along the coast, it becomes necessary to make the kind of intersite comparisons which involve relative evaluations. Some ecologists consider that with the pressures for coastal engineering works some form of prioritisation for designated sites (especially SSSIs) is essential if we accept that not all sites can be protected. An alternative view is that all Nature Conservation Review Grade 1 sites (Ratcliffe 1977), National Nature Reserves and sites of international importance should be regarded as 'inalienable' on a league table of grades of importance. Also that if SSSIs were of sufficient national importance to be designated in the first place then they should be treated as such by government policy in not allowing any engineering works or development without complete agreement from conservationists.

Overall, then, a number of reservations about the use of the matrix approach are apparent and should be borne in mind when it is applied to environmental decision-making. The issue of how to make between-site comparisons still remains, as does the question of how to consider 'ecological' values which reflect those of the public rather than professional ecologists. Such values would include the importance to the local population of a small and relatively undistinguished site in scientific terms which is highly valued by them for its educational and amenity use. Whereas the ecological matrix is not the medium for presenting such valuations, it is nevertheless essential that local communities are given an adequate opportunity to express formally such values in the course of the decision-making process and do not come to regard the use of the ecological matrices as a way of excluding consideration of public values.

References

Ratcliffe, D. A. (ed.) (1977) *A Nature Conservation Review Vol. 1*, Cambridge: Cambridge University Press.

Clayton, K.M. (1989) Implications of climate change. *Coastal Management: proceedings of the conference organized by the Institution of Civil Engineers and held in Bournemouth on 9–11 may 1989*, 227–41. London: Thomas Telford.

Gubbay, S. (1988) *A Coastal Directory for Marine Nature Conservation*, Ross-on-Wye: Marine Conservation Society.

10 Conclusions

C. Richards, C. H. Green and A. Coker

The main objective of this volume has been to identify areas of common ground amongst those with many different interests in valuing the coastline: for its ecological, geological and archaeological characteristics, for its recreational and amenity uses and for the development of coast protection and sea defence schemes. It is intended that this debate will be a contribution to the discussions of how far techniques of environmental evaluation and economic valuation are appropriate, the extent to which they have already been developed and some possible directions for further methodological development.

What has emerged from the debate, and this in itself is useful, is that there are fundamental differences in values which 'drive' differences in views on which approach should be taken when evaluating the needs for coast protection and sea defence works. These values lead to different emphases and different approaches, and to attempt to create mechanistic decision-making systems which ignore these underlying value differences is liable to failure.

This final chapter highlights some of the areas of common ground and dissent within and between ecologists and economists involved with coastal management so that readers can better appreciate the nature of future debates about the environmental aspects of coast protection and sea defence works. Such better understanding should clarify where compromise is possible and where it is not, and lead to better decisions (even if those decisions are to do nothing). The following sections summarise first: the apparent areas of agreement and disagreement over approaches to environmental evaluation and the extent to which economic values should be given to environmental attributes. Second, we review the implications of these agreements and disagreements for the development of economic methods to aid decision-making, and third, review future research needed to fill some of the major gaps in both our theoretical understanding of the issues involved and the methodological developments that need to be made. Finally, we discuss significance of the procedure put forward in Chapter 6 and the matrix outlined in Chapter 7 in the decision-making process with regard to coast protection and sea defence schemes.

General areas of agreement and disagreement

Not withstanding increased environmental awareness, greater priority should be given to the environmental aspects of coast protection schemes and at an earlier stage in scheme development than at present.

It is clear that the present methods of relative evaluation of environmental benefits are less than adequate, and that methods of economic valuation are totally inadequate. Attempts so far to put an economic value on sites of ecological interest have usually resulted in only a minimum value. The intrinsic value of wildlife, in so far as it is not dependent on human use values, has been omitted altogether in the absence of any appropriate method for its measurement. It is clearly possible to put an economic value on an aspect of the human use of an area, such as its agricultural or recreational use as Turner, Bateman and Brooke have shown in Chapter 5 with agricultural production values. They have further demonstrated how, in the case of specially designated areas such as ESAs, management payments may be used as proxy values for society's willingness to protect wildlife interests. Tunstall and Coker (Chapter 6) have illustrated the application of Contingent Valuation Methods for assessing a site's recreational value and this approach was also adopted by Turner et al. for the Aldeburgh study. However, the use of such values cannot be taken to imply any notion of the non-use (or intrinsic) ecological value of the site. There is lack of agreement over how this as yet unquantified value – or rather, package of values – could be accounted for or whether attempts should even be made to provide *any* monetary evaluations for the non-use component. If the value of an ecological site can be regarded as a moral absolute then this could imply that some constraints should be placed on decisions based solely on economic values. As the authors of Chapter 2 point out, society should take seriously the view that 'environmental phemonena' – and this encompasses such components as wildlife habitats – have a value in their own right independent of human preferences.

Improvements to the consideration of ecological aspects in coast protection schemes could be made in several ways. Project design should be an appraisal-led process with analysis of the ecological effects of a scheme being carried out at the start of any proposals as part of this process. The most ecologically sound schemes should be proposed, wherever feasible, before considerable expenditure has been committed to ecologically unacceptable designs. The ecological acceptability of any proposal would therefore be ensured before other aspects of its effects were considered. Benefit-cost analyses would then be carried out on the most environmentally favourable schemes overall.

For an assessment of a site's ecological value, the most up-to-date information available is required. This is necessary not only for accurate analysis of the current ecological situation and predictions of change, but also because with increased development at the coast, those sites which remain will be of increasing value.

Greater attention should be given to the future situation without a coast protection scheme: the 'do-nothing' option. Since coastal processes are dynamic, change – including habitat creation and habitat destruction – is an integral part of coastal ecology. Allowing the continuation of natural processes, the 'do-nothing' option may therefore be the most desirable option from an ecological point of view although this would have to be set against wider environmental considerations. Discussion of the Aldeburgh and Hengistbury Head schemes emphasised the importance of identifying the 'do nothing' condition. Both cases, with hindsight, raise the issue that erosion might have resulted in environmental benefits, rather than only the dis-benefits foreseen when the analyses were undertaken. Definition of future conditions without a scheme requires that the nature of the changes which would occur in that situation can be predicted, before a decision can be reached as to whether such changes are desirable.

The regional impacts of any proposed scheme should also be considered, as downdrift sites may be affected by loss of sediment, and first lines of defence, such as beaches and salt-marshes, may be lost elsewhere. Many of the present problems of coast protection have been caused by earlier protection schemes not taking into account regional coastal processes. The present situation of different coast protection authorities responsible for short stretches of coast, with the National Rivers Authority responsible for sea defence (i.e. against sea flooding), does not encourage the adequate integration of policy in regional terms.

There is not only a confusing complexity of different authorities involved with coast protection and sea defence, but also a number of different statutory procedures involved. Coast protection schemes arc not covered by environmental impact assessment (EIA) legislation unless they have 'significant' environmental effect. When coast protection schemes require planning permission, a coast protection authority may also be the planning authority and can grant itself planning permission for a scheme. In the absence of adequately integrated coastal zone management, a consultation procedure such as that proposed in Chapter 7 is required to ensure a way in which the ecological interests of a site can be fully taken into account in the decision-making process.

A number of areas of disagreement persist. First, over whether the economic valuation of ecological sites is valid. John Adams (Chapter 4), in particular, cautioned against the production of any kind of numbers, whether absolute economic values or relative ecological evaluations, which may only cover up underlying conflicts in fundamental values. A common view among economists is that the placing of a monetary value on wildlife is mainly a question of developing an appropriate methodology. On the other hand, Colin Green points out in Chapter 3 that the key issue is whether the underlying theory is adequate for the measurement to be valid when applied to non-use values. On the whole, ecologists feel that existing methods of ecological valuation omit too many aspects of that 'package of values' to provide an adequate quantification. In view of the complex nature of ecosystems and the various functions they perform, any attempts to develop a realistic valuation are likely to be extremely difficult.

There is also no common agreement over whether economic valuation of ecological sites is even desirable. On the whole, economists feel that ecological values could be more easily compared with other aspects of valuation if the same basis for measurement is used, i.e. money values. In contrast, many ecologists feel that, as a low priority is sometimes given by society to sites which scientific ecologists consider important, e.g. saltmarshes, an inadequate valuation would inevitably be placed on them. The inclusion of environmental *information* about a site was felt to be of greater priority than attempting to produce a monetary valuation of doubtful validity.

Another area of disagreement is whether site prioritisation should be attempted. Economists and some ecologists think that, as it is not even possible to protect all of the designated sites in practice, a further system of site prioritisation should be developed, in particular with regard to Sites of Special Scientific Interest (SSSIs). An alternative view is that designations of national and international value (including SSSIs) should be respected as such and that all these sites should be 'sacrosanct': that by selecting these sites for statutory designation, the government has acknowledged their value and should provide a firmer framework to ensure they are adequately protected.

The habitat criteria matrix proposed by Cathy Richards in Chapter 8 as a method for summarising ecological change can be seen to have both advantages and limitations. In the view of many economists, it would be of greater use in site assessment terms if the visual indicators could be converted into a monetary value, or at least could be replaced by numbers. From this viewpoint, the matrices could be seen as a route to economic valuation, rather than used for summarising relative ecological value. From an ecological perspective the matrices could provide a useful summary of the reasons for the value of a site although some may think that site value cannot be adequately summarised by such an inevitable simplification. Overall, if the matrices are to be used at all then their limitations should be stressed: that is, their use should be restricted to comparison of changes at a particular site and within an appraisal-led approach to scheme development.

It is clear that the role of any ecological appraisal should be to inform the political decision-making processes concerned with coastal and other developments affecting the environment. A key problem area remains how to negotiate the trade-offs between beneficial ecological impacts and negative impacts such as upon archaeological sites. If a coast protection scheme were to be desirable upon environmental grounds, then the use value of affected sites could also be counted among the benefits. However, if these use values are in themselves insufficient to justify a scheme which is still desirable on ecological grounds, the inability to quantify this ecological value will still be a stumbling block in any decision-making process and must be recognised as such. Decision-makers should be made aware that ecologists are often more concerned with wider ecological impacts, both direct and indirect, of coast protection schemes rather than with mere habitat or species 'protection'.

Both governmental and non-governmental agencies were invited to submit statements after the workshop. The following is a summary of the RSPB view of decision-making as it affects land drainage, flood defence, sea defence and coastal protection schemes.

The workshop was in part based on the premise that cost-benefit analysis (CBA) was the primary decision-making process, and that by including environmental intangibles, better decision-making will result. That ignores the reality of political expediency, the fact that projects are promoted irrespective of economic efficiency (financial benefits to individuals motivate many improvement works or development schemes) and recent legislative developments in environmental impact assessment. The latter has the potential to have the most profound effect upon CBA procedures operated by government.

The RSPB propose that the primary decision-making process in land drainage, flood defence and coast protection schemes should be the EIA. The CBA should only be used to make the decision upon whether or not to grant aid the option identified by the EIA with minimum or zero adverse impact upon the environment. Government grant aid should not be used to promote environmentally damaging schemes, however favourable the CBA. This assumes of course that the EIA is carried out correctly with full appraisal of the 'do nothing' option, etc. as discussed at the workshop.

The route suggested at the workshop of extending the CBA to include valuation of 'uses' of the environment and presentation of externalities and intangibles in the form of a matrix is effectively a CBA with summary EIA. The RSPB does not object to the valuation of 'uses' in the CBA, as described in the case histories at the workshop, although disagreements will arise over the methodologies on occasions (e.g. the inconsistent approach at Aldeburgh). It is the unknown weight given by the decision-maker to the proposed matrix which gives rise to concern. It would be better to present the decision-maker with the full EIA appraisal of options rather than the summary matrix appended to the CBA. If primacy is given to assessment of the environmental impacts during option appraisal, and CBA conducted upon the environmentally benign options, then assessment of intangibles as part of the CBA becomes superfluous.

In summary, primacy should be given to the EIA over CBA in the decision-making process.

The following is a statement received from Dr Pat Doody, Head of Coastal Ecology Branch, Chief Scientist's Directorate, Nature Conservancy Council (since 1.4.91: English Nature).

The development of procedures for evaluating areas of importance for nature conservation is a long established practice. In particular the Guidelines for the selection of biological Sites of Special Scientific Interest (Nature Conservancy Council 1989) set out the rationale, operational approach and criteria for identifying the most important wildlife sites in Great Britain. These Guidelines provide a detailed breakdown of habitat and vegetation types. For example, there are 22 selection units in the four main coastal habitats: sand dunes, shingle, saltmarshes and sea-cliffs.

Given the complexity of natural and semi-natural systems which is reflected in the guidelines, the problem of using a matrix involving habitats, of the kind outlined at the workshop, is one of gross over-simplification of the true situation. As such it cannot give an adequate representation of the value of the ecological resource. To then assign economic values which themselves only provide a partial answer to the valuation process, leaves a considerable amount of uncertainty.

The examples that were used to aid discussion assumed that the existing conservation interest within the sites should be protected, thus reinforcing, in both cases, the argument for protective measures based on engineering principles. Although a majority of wildlife sites, notably SSSIs, should be considered sacrosanct as far as destructive development is concerned, that is not to say that change cannot be accommodated within them. This is particularly true when change – as represented by the mobility of tides and sediments or the accretion and erosion of saltmarshes and sand dunes – is part of the natural process of habitat development. It should also be remembered that protection defined in engineering terms of one site may have knock-on effects which may not be in the best interests of adjacent areas. Under these circumstances, even assuming the economic valuations of the existing ecological features is adequate, there may be other scenarios or factors which should be taken into account.

Returning to the habitat classification matrix, even at the superficial level proposed, this should incorporate a number of changes. For example, dune systems could be further classified according to the nature of the sand (calcareous and acidic); similar rock types vary considerably in geological terms which has a profound effect on vegetation types, as does the stability of the system. Grazing management of all habitats on the coast is crucial to their interest, and saltmarshes in particular show major swings in the type of conservation importance depending on the scale and intensity of grazing pressure.

Overall it is felt that the best that any evaluation system can do in economic terms is to provide a check-list of things to look for and features of special note. Given that the complex procedures for site evaluation attempt to take account of the complexities, including management considerations, of habitats and species concentration, this should form the starting point for any economic evaluation of areas of biological (or geological/geomorphological) significance. We must recognise the importance of sites which are identified through existing conservation legislation and assign these a priority commensurate with their national or international importance.

Economic issues

The problems associated with economic discounting were outlined in the discussion in Chapter 3. The general principle of discounting and the question of intergenerational equity were highlighted as particularly problematic. The adequacy of the theoretical basis of discounting, and especially the concept of social time preference, was questioned and found wanting. Intergenerational equity was considered to be an issue which could only be included in benefit-cost analyses as a constraint. In general, it is clear that the value of environmental assets increases over time and if economic measures are going to be used at all, this growth ought to be incorporated in benefit-cost analyses.

Part of the objection to the inclusion of environmental goods in economic analyses arises from a belief that the economic assumption that one form of consumption can be substituted for any other form of consumption is incorrect. This is particularly important where what is being considered is the irreversible loss of a form of natural capital.

Designated sites, such as SSSIs in particular, are regarded by many as inalienable. Some ecologists feel that the intrinsic value of these sites imposes an onus on anyone proposing to alter the site to justify that interference. From this perspective, it is unlikely that any form of monetary valuation would be considered an appropriate procedure for establishing adequate justification.

As discussed in this volume, then, the overall impression is that economic analysis, as a form of project appraisal, has failed to date to fulfil one of the main criteria for any form of project appraisal: that of clarifying the issues where ecological interests are involved.

It is clear that we have not yet succeeded, in any but the most general way, in quantifying many of the use values associated with the total package of ecological values of a site. For example, it is difficult to anticipate and hence to value the importance for environmental monitoring. It is especially difficult to begin to evaluate the non-use values of the environment such as the ecological role of a site, in contributing to the stability of adjacent natural systems and there is little reason for confidence in our abilities to quantify these non-use values in the near future. Before methods for assessing non-use values can be developed, some fundamental theoretical economic issues relating to the nature of public choice and individual preference will have to be addressed.

In contrast, there is some confidence in the application of Contingent Valuation Methods to assess the use values of a site, in particular recreational use. Although this technique is still in its developmental stage, many believe that it can become a valid and reliable method for quantifying use values.

In this respect we need to remember that economics, in a similar way to mathematics, seeks to build rigorous analysis upon some set of axioms. Unlike mathematics, the validity of economic analysis ultimately depends upon whether the axioms adopted adequately reflect generally held moral values. Consequently, it is open to any society to choose the axiomatic basis to be adopted.

Future research needs

Research needs can, therefore, be grouped into two categories: first, theoretical issues which relate to the validity of the assumptions embodied in a particular system of economic analysis, and second, methodological issues to improve the rigour of the analysis.

At the *theoretical* level, research needs are to examine whether the Potential Pareto Improvement criterion adequately reflects public beliefs as to the basis upon which decisions about the provision of public goods should be undertaken; to investigate the content and functional form of the individual's utility function, including the degree to which altruistic or moral concerns as well as pure self-interest are included. The assumption in economics that values are solely given by the individual, rather than there being any intrinsic or social values, needs to be tested. Even when intergenerational equity issues are accepted as a constraint, the degree to which the preferences for consumption as distributed over time can be adequately approximated by the use of a discount rate requires further consideration. In the UK context, estimation of the opportunity cost of capital as an economic return, after taking out externalities as well as transfer payments, needs further work. Finally, the validity of the economic assumption that consumption of any one good is more or less substitutable by consumption of any other good needs to be tested.

At a *methodological* level, research requirements include the development of criteria which clearly relate to the use-value of environmental sites (e.g. as gene pools, environmental monitors, etc.); the development of methods to estimate the use values of environmental sites; the determination of public preferences for environmental site conservation, including the public's criteria for the importance of different sites; the determination of the validity and reliability of the CVM and the best practice in its use; and the estimation of growth rates for the values of environmental sites reflecting the income and supply elasticity for these goods.

Conclusion

If we accept that it is not helpful to develop further methods for quantifying environmental value, and that the 'messy politics' approach to decision advocated by Adams is preferable, then the issue becomes what is the best way of expressing environmental values so that they can be easily used in decision-making. It is clearly a more complex task to express these values in terms of society's collective reasons for valuing them than it is to present them in a numerical form. But if such quantification is in reality no more than 'pseudo-evaluation', that is a measure of what is most easily quantified rather than what is held most important, then it does not advance the consideration of underlying environmental values in decision-making – it only appears to do so. Through systematisation of the consultation process as outlined in Chapter 7, we have now devised a mechanism for the implicit valuation of environmental resources in the decision-making process. This is more than simply advocating wider consultation since the process of informed trade-offs is the mechanism by which values are expressed. In other words, it can be seen as the systematisation of 'messy politics'.

Appendix

List of Speakers

John Adams
Department of Geography, University College, London
Ian Bateman
Environmental Appraisal group, University of East Anglia
Alan Holland
Department of Philosophy, Lancaster University
Annabel Coker
Flood Hazard Research Centre
Colin Green
Flood Hazard Research Centre
Cathy Richards
Flood Hazard Research Centre
Sylvia Tunstall
Flood Hazard Research Centre

List of Delegates

Roger Buisson
Royal Society for the Protection of Birds
Nigel Clark
British Trust for Ornithology, Tring
Pat Doody
Nature Conservancy Council, Peterborough
Alan A. Fearn
Ministry of Agriculture, Fisheries and Food, London
Susan Gubbay
Marine Conservation Society, Ross-on-Wye
Richard Hobbs
Norfolk Naturalist Trust, Norwich
Nigel Holmes
Environmental Consultatnt, Warboys, Cambs.
Margaret House
Flood Hazard Research Centre

Alan Mckirdy
Nature Conservancy Council, Peterborough
Ronan Palmer
Department of the Environment, London
Edmund Penning-Rowsell
Flood Hazard Research Centre
Richard Scott
Institute of Terrestrial Ecology, Grange-over-Sands, Cumbria
Paul Thompson
Flood Hazard Research Centre
Ray Woolmore
Countryside Commission, Cheltenham
Tim Yates
Ministry of Agriculture, Fisheries and Food, London

Index